SUBSIDIA BIBLICA

21

subsidia biblica – 21

ROBERT NORTH, S.J.

Bibliography

1936 - 2002

EDITRICE PONTIFICIO ISTITUTO BIBLICO — ROMA 2001

ISBN 88-7653-616-7

© E.P.I.B. – Roma – 2001

Iura editionis et versionis reservantur

EDITRICE PONTIFICIO ISTITUTO BIBLICO

Piazza della Pilotta, 35 - 00187 Roma, Italia

Bibliography 1936-2002
superseding all four previous partial editions

1273 titles, counting in
138 variants: editions, reprints, comments
219 separate books in multiple-review bulletins
335 brief excavation reports in surveys

Books
AUTHORS
Articles, *Periodicals*
subjects
Others' Books reviewed
terms, Hebrew/Greek
archeological sites

PREFACE

We here present the bibliography of one of our illustrious professors, Rev. Robert Grady North, S.J., Professor Emeritus of Archeology and Geography at the Pontifical Biblical Institute. Fr. North's publications are numerous. Unlike many Jesuits, Fr. North did not wait until he had finished his terminal degree before he began publishing; and his ability in so many languages and academic fields and his remarkable skill at gathering and organizing all types of data allowed him to publish over an extremely wide range of topics. From travelogues and book reviews, he soon moved to archeology and exegesis. His doctorate on the Jubilee brought out its intimate relation to the Ezra-era and even to Maccabees; and Fr. North has continued to study these themes, as is evident from his two latest books in the series Analecta Biblica (nn.142 and 145) in the year 2000. He has written on the history and religions of Egypt and Mesopotamia and participated in excavations in the Bible-lands, a continuing account of which was invited by the Catholic Biblical Quarterly. This participation in various excavations, like that at Ghassul, and his study tours of these and other sites led to many published reports and detailed explanations and documentations as well as to a famous series of slides. These academic labors proved all the more interesting since Fr. North, a pioneer at heart, had an uncanny ability to reach almost inaccessible areas and, of course, to come away with the right photo and with a font of information of interest to all.

More recently, Fr. North has written articles for encyclopedias and contributed to Festschriften in honor of the countless scholars whose friendship and esteem he has gained during his long academic career. Even as professor emeritus, Fr. North still had exceptional energy and productivity, as his editorship of the *Elenchus of Biblica* from 1979 to 1995 well demonstrates.

Both friends and scholars in the various biblical fields will find in this bibliography easy reference to all of Fr. North's publications. Their number and quality leave no doubt about his contribution to the study of the Bible and related specializations.

Rev. Prof. Robert F. O'Toole, S.J.
Rector, Pontifical Biblical Institute

R. North Bibliography 1936-2002

N° 1 Telemachus – the "Juvenile Lead", *Classical Bulletin* 12/4 (Jan. 1936) 29-30.

2 **The Platonic Protagoras**: dissertation. St. Louis University, Feb. 1939.

3 LIVINGSTONE R.W., *Portrait of Socrates* (Oxford 1938): [R]*Classical Bulletin* 15/5 (Mar. 1939) 48.

4 Humanism in Education, *Thought* 15/54 (Sept. 1939) 401-412.

5 Eagle not of Earth (a sonnet on PINDAR), *Classical Bulletin* 16/1 (Oct. 1939) 4.

6 **The General who Rebuilt the Jesuits**, a biography of John ROOTHAAN: Science and Culture Series, ed. Joseph HUSSLEIN Milwaukee 1944, Bruce. xii-292 p.-- [R]MCNASPY C., *Review for Religious* 3,4 (1944)352

7 Scripture in the Christmas Liturgy, *Review for Religious* 3/4 (Oct. 1944) 368-376. [Book-reviews on *Joshua, The Popes.* etc. ...]

8 **The Inhabitation Controversy in Cyril of Alexandria**: St. Louis University theology licentiate thesis. St Marys KA 1945. 57 p., typed.

9 **All-Stars of Christ**, biographies of young men. Milwaukee 1946, Bruce. x-187 p.

10 Liturgy's Grandest Display: a Saint's Canonization, *Action Now* 1/8 (St. Louis Apr.1948) 9f.

N° 11   Festival in France: Thousands Acclaim the Queen Mother in her Brittany Bower, *Action Now* 2/1 (Oct.1948) 6-7.

11a   Scenario for Life (experiences of a young social worker in postwar Rhineland), *Social Order* 1/10 (St. Louis, Dec.1948) 433-6.

12 Day of Glory in Cologne: Catholic Germany (rebuilt cathedral dedication), *Action Now* 2/2 (Nov.1948) 3-4.

13   "And Thou, Capharnaum ...", *American Ecclesiastical Review* 121/5 (Nov. 1949) 373-379.

14   Beth-Shan and Megiddo, *Catholic Biblical Quarterly* 12/1 (Jan. 1950) 84-89.

15   Arabs in Palestine: the Problem of Arab Refugees, *Social Order* 23/3 (Mar.1950) 99-104.

16   Thronus Satanae pergamenus, *Verbum Domini* 28/2 (Mar. 1950) 65-76.

17 JUVENAL's Exile, *Classical Bulletin* 26/5 (Mar.1950) 49-52.

18   Longe clarissimum Asiae Pergamum, *Classical Bulletin* 26/6 (Apr.1950) 63-71.

19   "Humilis corde" in luce Psalmorum, *Verbum Domini* 28/3 (May 1950) 153-161.

19a ... digested in Johannes BAUER, Theologie der Psalmen: Armut, *Bibel und Liturgie* 21 (1953) 34-35.

20 Flight into Egypt 1950, *Queen's Work* 42/4 (Jan.1950) p. 3-5.

21   Mary's Last Home, *American Ecclesiastical Review* 123/4 (Oct. 1950) 242-261.
21a ...   reprinted in FENTON (J.) & BENARD, *Studies in Praise of our Blessed Mother* (Washington DC 1952) 171-190.

22   Biblical Echoes in the Holy Year, *American Ecclesiastical Review* 123/6 (Dec.1950) 416-436.

23   Survey of *Zeitschrift für die alttestamentliche Wissenschaft* 62 (1949-50) in *Verbum Domini* 29/1 (Feb.1951) 46-50.

24   Survey of *Judaica* 6 (1950) in *Verbum Domini* 29/1(Jan.1951)50-53

25   ARCE Augustín, *Miscelánea de Tierra Santa* (Jerusalem 1950): [R]*Verbum Domini* 29/1 (Jun.1951) 189-190.

26   The Biblical Jubilee and Social Reform, *Scripture* 4/11 (Jul.1951) 189-190.

27   **Historia excavationis biblicae**: mimeographed Latin lectures on each leading excavator linked to a major site in chronological order. Rome 1951, Pontifical Biblical Institute. 25 p.

28   Prophetismus ut philosophia historiae, *Verbum Domini* 29/6 (Dec.1951) 321-333.

29   *New World Translation of the Christian Greek Scriptures* (Brooklyn 1950): [R]*Verbum Domini* 30/2 (Apr.1952) 121-122.

30   Moses and the Average Priest, *American Ecclesiastical Review* 126/4 (Apr. 1952) 241-257.
30a ... Pentateuch-origins bibliography reprinted by J. Coppens in *Ephemerides Theologicae Lovanienses* 28 (1952) 537-9.

N° 31   CORBO Virgilio, ed., *Custodia di Terra Santa 1342-1942* (Jerusalem 1951): [R]*Verbum Domini* 30/2 (Mar. 1952) 122-124.

32   NEUVILLE René, *Paléolithique et mésolithique* [[R]wrongly *néolithique*] *du désert de Judée* (Paris1951): [R]*Proche-Orient Chrétien* 2 (1952) 188-190; rejoinder 290!

33   **Descriptio terrae biblicae:** zones of visit; also hydrography, flora, geopolitics. Rome 1952, Pontificial Biblical Institute. 25 p.

Nº 34 Leviticus expositus et exponendus [on W.E. GISPEN, *Het boek Leviticus*: AALDERS Comm.; Kampen 1950; 403 p.): [R]*Verbum Domini* 30/5 (Oct. 1952) 278-288.

35 RÚIZ GARCÍA Samuel [later famed Mexico bishop], Iter syrojordanicum1952 [North's first], *Verbum Domini* 37/1 (Jan. 1953) 3-12.

36 The 1952 [KENYON] Jericho-Sultan Excavation,*Biblica* 34/1 (Jan. 1953) 1-12.

37 WISCHNITZER Rachel, *Messianic Themes in the Dura Synagogue* (Chicago 1948): [R]*Biblica* 34/1 (Jan. 1953) 111-112.

38 Leeds Excavation at Jaffa, *Biblica* 34/1 (Jan. 1953) 121.

39 SIMONS J., *Jerusalem in the Old Testament* (Leiden 1952): [R]*Biblica* 34/2 (1953) 224-235.

40 MARMARDJI A.-S., *Textes géographiques arabes* (Paris 1951): [R]*Orientalia* 22/3 (Jul. 1953) 320-322.

41 El nuevo "santuario" de Jericó, *Estudios Eclesiásticos* 27/3 (Jul. 1953) 325-337.

42 SCHECHTMAN Joseph B., *The Arab Refugee Problem* (New York 1952): [R]*Social Order* 3 (1953) 139-140.

43 VILNAY Zev, *Madrik Ereṣ Yisra'el* (Guide to Palestine; Jerusalem 1946-50): [R]*Biblica* 34/3 (Jul. 1953) 405-411.

44 RIIS P.J., *Hama, les cimetières à crémation* (Copenhagen 1948): [R]*Biblica* 34/3 (Jul. 1953) 411-412.

45 HENNINGER Joseph, *Rites de printemps chez les Arabes* (São Paulo 1950): [R]*Biblica* 34/3 (Jul. 1953) 412.

46 DETWEILER A. Henry, *Manual of Archeological Surveying* (New Haven 1948): [R]*Biblica* 34/3 (Jul. 1953) 412.

47 JEREMIAS Joachim, *Die Wiederentdeckung von Bethesda* (Göttingen 1949): [R]*Biblica* 34/3 (Jul.1953) 412.

48 *Millon l'munne ha-qaddarût* (Dictionary of ceramic terms: Jerusalem 1950): [R]*Biblica* 34/3 (1953) 413-414.

49 DUNAND Maurice, *Byblia grammata* (Beirut 1945): [R]Biblica 34/3 (Jul.1953) 412-413.

50 **Stratigraphia Palaestinae** (each successive period highlighted by its most conspicuous excavation). Rome 1953, Pontifical Biblical Institute. 53 p.

50a .... revised [2]1954.

51 Maccabean Sabbath Years, *Biblica* 34/4 (1953) 501-515.

52 AUGUSTINOVIĆ Agostino, *Gerico e dintorni: guida* (Jerusalem 1951): [R]Biblica 34/4 (Oct.1953) 541-3.

N° 53 POIDEBARD A. & LAUFFRAY J., *Sidon* (Beirut 1951): [R]*Biblica* 34/4 (Oct.1953) 543.

54 GLUECK Nelson, *Explorations* [not `excavations', [R]title mistake] *in Eastern Palestine* IV: ASOR Annual 25-28 for 1945-9 (New Haven 1951): [R]*Biblica* 34/4 (Oct.1953) 547-551.

55 Biblical and Archeological News, *Catholic Biblical Quarterly* 16/1 (Jan.1954) 33-37: 33 Siloam; 34 Beersheba, Beit-Shearim, Dothan; 35 Jericho, Qumran, Bethlehem; 36 Dhiban, Cyprus, Boghazköy.

56 Current Palestine Prehistory (four surveyed together; RUST apart), *Biblica* 35/1 (Jan.1954) 80-88:

56a ALIMEN H., *Atlas de préhistoire* (Paris 1950) 80-85.

56b LEROI-GOURHAN A., *Les fouilles préhistoriques* (Paris 1950) 80-85

[N° 56 Prehistory] c NEUVILLE René, *Le paléolithique et le mésolithique* [not "néolithique" as N° 32] *du désert de Judée* (Paris 1951) 83-85.

56d OAKLEY K., *Man the Tool-Maker*[2] (London 1952) 81-85.

56e RUST A., *Die Höhlenfunde von Jabrud* (Neumünster 1950) 86-88.

57 Explorationes archaeologicae Palaestinae 1953, *Biblica* 35,1 (Jan.1954) 139-141: 139 Dothan; Beit-Shearim; 140 Dhiban; 141 Bethlehem, Beit-Yera, Negev.

58 *Eretz-Israel Annual 1* (Jerusalem 1951): [R]*Verbum Domini* 32/1 (Feb. 1954) 43-45.

59 ABEL F.-M., *Histoire de la Palestine depuis .. Alexandre* (Paris 1952): [R]*Biblica* 35/2 (Apr.1954) 246-7.

60 ABEL F.-M., *Livres des Maccabées* (Paris 1949): [R]Biblica 35/2 (Apr.1954) 247-9.

61 SCHNEIDER Hilary, *Memorial of Moses on Mt. Nebo III. Pottery* (Jerusalem 1950): [R]*Biblica* 35/2 (Apr.1954) 249-251.

62 SALLER S. & BAGATTI B., *Town of Nebo* (Mekhayyat; Jerusalem 1949): [R]*Biblica* 35/2 (Apr.1954) 250.

63 SURIANO F., ed. BELLORINI T. & HOADE E., *Treatise on the Holy Land* (Jerusalem 1949): [R]*Biblica* 35/2 (Apr.1954) 250-251.

64a MOLDENKE H.& A., *Plants of the Bible* (Waltham 1952): [R]*Biblica* 35/2 (Apr.1954) 255.

64b EIG N. & FEINBRUNN N., *Magdir* (Analytical Flora of Palestine), *Iconographia florae terrae Israelis* (Jerusalem 1952): [R]*Biblica* 35/2 (Apr.1954) 255.

65 Conventus societatis anglicae studiorum V.T., *Biblica* 35/2 (Apr.1954) 261-263.

66 Troglodytae ghassuliani prope Beeršeba, *Biblica* 35/2 (Apr.1954) 272.

67 *Bamôt* arte factae tempore Josiae?, *Biblica* 35/2 (Apr.1954) 272-273.

68 Israel's Tribes and Today's Frontier, *Catholic Biblical Quarterly* 16/2 (Apr.1954) 146-153.

69 Winter Meeting of the British Society for Old Testament Study, *Catholic Biblical Quarterly* 16/2 (Apr.1954) 191-2.

70 MURRAY John (paper in seminar of North), Instrumenta musica S. Scripturae, *Verbum Domini* 12/2 (Apr.1954) 84-89; fig.

N° 71 *Yad* in the Shemitta-Law, *Vetus Testamentum* 4/2 (Apr.1954) 196-9.

72 **Sociology of the Biblical Jubilee**: Analecta Biblica 4, Rome 1954, Pontifical Biblical Institute, S.S.D. dissertation (Lev 25 an elsewhere biblically attested early synthesis of social-justice legislation, especially against permanent enslavement or property-alienation as effect of bankruptcy) xlvi-245 p. → N° 580 below..

Scholarly reviews:

72a ALBRIGHT W., *Biblica* 37/4 (Oct.1956) 488-490.

72b ASENSIO F., *Gregorianum* 37/2 (Apr.1956) 300.

72c BARDTKE H., *Orientalistische Literaturzeitung* 59 (1956) 239-241.

72d CAZELLES H., *Vetus Testamentum* 5/3 (Jul.1955) 321-324.

72e COPPENS J., *Ephemerides Theologicae Lovanienses* 30 (1954) 747-9.

72f DOWD W., *Theological Studies* 18/3 (Jul.1955) 436-438.

72g HASPECKER J., *Scholastik* 31/3 (Jul.1956) 424-5.

72h HEMPEL J., *Zeitschrift für die alttestamentliche Wissenschaft* 66/3 (1954) 292f.

72i JIRKU A., *Deutsche Literaturzeitung* 76/3 (Mar.1955) 165-166

72j ŁACH S. in Polish

72k LAMBERT Gustav, *Nouvelle Revue Théologique* 77/6 (Jun.1955) 30-1.

72L LOEWENSTAMM S., *Beth Mikra* L/1 (Apr.1958) 27-28.

72m MENDELSOHN L., *Journal of Biblical Literature* 75/3 (Jul.1956) 262-4.

N° 72n RAVENNA A., *Rassegna Mensile d'Israele* 21 (1955) 255-6.

72ö ROWLEY H., *Expository Times* 67/4 (Jan.1956); SOTS *Book List* (1955) 53.

72p DE VAUX Roland, *Revue Biblique* 62/4 (Oct.1955) 610-612.

72q VAWTER Bruce, *Catholic Biblical Quarterly* 17/3 (Jul.1955) 513-515.

73 A Refuge of the Sanhedrin, *Scripture* 6 (1954) 169=174: Beit-Shearim.

74 Dibon prout effossione innotescit, *Biblica* 35/3 (Jul.1954) 402-404.

75 Recentiores explorationes prope Jericho, *Biblica* 35/3 (Jul,1954) 404, Qumran.

76 Qumran and its Archeology, *Catholic Biblical Quarterly* 16/3 (July 1954) 426-437.

77 Biblical and Archeological News, *Catholic Biblical Quarterly* 16/3 (Jul 1954)219-326: 319 Qumran; Olivet, Dominus Flevit; 320 Jericho-Sultân; 322 Beersheba; Ora; 323 Rephaim; 324 Famagusta, Salamis, Ugarit; 325 Giza.

78 Recent Catholic Biblical Aids, *Gregorianum* 35/3 (Jul 1954) 506-511:
                                        survey:
78a AUVRAY P., *Ézéchiel* (Paris 1949): 506.

78b *Catholic Family Edition of the Bible* (New York 1953): 511.

78c CLAMER A., *La Genêse* (Paris 1953) 511.

78d BONSIRVEN J. & TRICOT A. ed., *Crampon Ste Bible* (Paris 1952) 511.

78e DUESBERG H., *Proverbes* (Paris 1951).

78f JUNKER H., *Genesis* (Würzburg 1949).

78g LYONNET S., *Galates-Romains* (Paris 1953).

78h ORCHARD B., ed., [Nelson's] *Catholic Commentary on Holy Scripture* (London 1953) 505.

78i SCHNEIDER H., *2.-5. Buch Moses* (Würzburg 1952) 509.

78j TRINQUET J., *Habaquq* (Paris 1953) 510.

78k DE VAUX R., *Genèse* (Paris 1951) 510.

79 LAMING A., ed., *La découverte du passé* (Paris 1952): [R]*Orientalia* 28/3 (Jul.1954) 268-270.

80 DELOUGAZ Pinhas, *Pottery from the Diyala Region* (Chicago 1952) [R]*Orientalia* 28/3 (Jul.1954) 270-3.

81 SCHAEFFER Claude, *Enkomi-Alasia* (Paris 1952): [R]*Orientalia* 23/3 (Jul.1954) 274-276.

82 LATOR E., *Parlez-vous arabe?* (Beirut 1953): [R]*Orientalia* 23/3 (Jul.1954) 305-306.

83 YOUNG Edward J., *Arabic for Beginners*[2] (Grand Rapids 1953): [R]*Orientalia* 23/3 (Jul.1954) 306-307.

84 GUARDUCCI M., *Cristo e san Pietro in un documento pre-costantiniano della necropolis vaticana* (Rome 1953): [R]*Verbum Domini* 32/4 (Aug.1954) 244-247.

N° 85 Confraternity of Christian Doctrine, *Holy Bible I. Genesis to Ruth* (Paterson 1953): [R]*Biblica* 35/4 (Oct.1954) 512-513.

86 BIRNBAUM S., *Qumran Scrolls and Palaeography* (New Haven 1952): [R]*Orientalia* 23/4 (Oct.1954) 455-456.

87 BOWEN R., *Early Arabian Necropolis of Ain Jawan* (New Haven 1950): [R]*Orientalia* 23/4 (Oct.1954) 455-6.

88 SELLERS O., BARAMKI D., *Roman-Byzantine Burial Cave* [Sabastiya] (New Haven 1953): [R]*Orientalia* 23/4 (Oct.1954) 455-6.

89 MEYSELS T., SENÈS H., Les guides bleus: Israël (Paris 1953):[R]*Verbum Domini* 32/5 (Oct.1954) 307-308.

90 BALDI D., *Guida di Terra Santa* (Jerusalem 1953): [R]*Verbum Domini* 32/5 (Oct.1954) 308-309.

91 ERDMAN C., *Book of Leviticus* (New York 1951): [R]*Verbum Domini* 32/5 (Oct. 1954) 317.

92 KERN F., VALJAVEC F., *Historia Mundi II* (Berlin 1953): [R]*Verbum Domini* 32/6 (Dec.1954) 348-351.

93 RUMPF A., *Archäologie* (Berlin 1953): [R]*Verbum Domini* 32/6 (Dec. 1954) 367.

94 Excavated Materials and Syntheses, *Biblica* 36/1 (Jan.1955) 78-92;
survey.

94a BARROIS A., *Manuel d'archéologie biblique II* (Paris 1953) [R]83-85.

94b BOMAN T., *Das hebräische Denken im Vergleich mit dem Griechischen* (Göttingen 1952): [R]91-92.

N° 94c BROWN T., *Excavations in Azarbaijan 1948* (London 1951): [R]83.

94d CROSS F., FREEDMAN D., *Early Hebrew Orthography* (New Haven 1952): [R]90-91.

94e DIKAIOS P., *Guide to Cyprus Museum* (Nicosia 1953): [R]83.

94f DIKAIOS P., *Khirokitia 1936-1946* (London 1953): [R]81.

94g DRIVER G., *Hebrew Scrolls* (London 1951): [R]92.

94h DUSSAUD R., *Prélydiens, Hittites et Achéens* (Paris 1953): [R]89-90.

94i FREE J., *Archaeology and Bible History* (Wheaton IL 1952): [R]86-87.

94j GORDON Cyrus, *Introduction to Old Testament Times* (Ventnor 1953): [R]85-86.

94k HARDING G.L., *Four Tomb Groups* (Ḥuṣn, ʿAmman, Madaba; London 1953): [R]81.

94L MILLER M.& J., *Harper's Bible Dictionary* (New York 1952): [R]89.

94m PARROT A., *La tour de Babel* (Neuchâtel 1953): [R]90.

94n TUFNELL O., *Lachish III* (London 1953): [R]78-80.

95 ABEL F.M., *Josué* (Paris 1950): [R]*Biblica* 36/1 (Jan.1955) 96-97

96 CAZELLES H., *Lévitique-Nombres-Deutéronome* (Paris 1952): [R]Biblica 36/1 (Jan.1955) 95-96.

97 COUROYER B., *Exode* (Paris 1952): [R]*Biblica* 36/1 (Jan.1955) 94-95.

98 DEVAUX R., *Genèse* (Paris 1951): [R]*Biblica* 36/1 (Jan.1955) 93-94.

99 Domus Petri, domus Domini, domus Patris, *Biblica* 36/1 (Jan.1955) 156.

100 Biblical and Archeological News, *Catholic Biblical Quarterly* 17/1 (Jan.1955) 25-33: Qumran 25; Quruntal, Tirṣa, Bethel 26; Nazareth, Netopa, Ramat Raḥel 27; Nahariya, `En-Gedi 28; Dor, Ascalon 29; Atlit, Giza 30; Spina 31; Knossos 32.

101 Metallurgy in the Ancient Near East, [R]article on R.J. FORBES, *Metallurgy in Antiquity* (Leiden 1950): *Orientalia* 24/1 (Jan.1955) 78-88.

102 ZIEGLER C., *Die Keramik von der Qal`a des Ḥaǧǧi Mohammed* (Berlin 1953): [R]*Orientalia* 24,1 (Jan.1955) 108.

103 AWAD Hassan, *La montagne du Sinaï central* (Cairo 1951): [R]*Orientalia* 24/1 (Jan.1955) 109-110.

104 The Damascus of Qumran Geography, *Palestine Exploration Quarterly* 87/1 (Jan.1955) 34-48 (omitted in their index-volume).

105 DELCOR M., *Manuscrits de la mer Morte: Midrash d'Habaquq* (Paris 1951): [R]*Verbum Domini* 33/1 (Jan.1955) 52.

106 AUERBACH Elias, *Moses* (Amsterdam 1953): [R]*Verbum Domini* 33/1 (Jan.1955) 56-58.

107 *Monumentum epigraphiae israelianae* (for A. REIFENBERG, Jerusalem 1954): [R]*Biblica* 36/2 (Jan.1955) 152-3.

108 Templum Nahariya et varia archaeologica, *Biblica* 6/1 (Jan.1955) 153-6; Tirṣa, Bethel, Nazareth 154; Ascalon 155.

109 The Derivation of Sabbath, *Biblica* 36/2 (Apr 1955) 182-201.

110 The Qumran "Sadducees" [O'HARA Fest. 44-68 =] *Catholic Biblical Quarterly* 17/2 (Apr.1955) 164-168.

111 SCHMIDT Erich F., *Persepolis I* (Chicago 1953): ^{R}*Orientalia* 24/2 (Apr.1955) 185-188.

112 L.-H. VINCENT, *Jérusalem de l'Ancien Testament* (Paris 1954): ^{R}*Orientalia* 14/2 (April 1955) 188-195.

113 KUBLER K., *Kerameikos* (Athens: Berlin 1954): ^{R}*Orientalia* 24/2 (Apr 1955) 195-197.

114 PARROT A., *Golgotha et Saint-Sépulcre* (Neuchâtel 1955): ^{R}*Orientalia* 25/2 (Apr 1955) 204-205.

115 NOTH Martin, *Das Buch Josue*^{2} (Tübingen 1953): ^{R}*Verbum Domini* 33/2 (Apr. 1955) 109-110.

116 Flesh, Covering, and Response, Ex xxi 10: *Vetus Testamentum* 5/2 (Apr.1955) 204-206.

117 BRESSAN Gino, *Samuele* (Torino 1952): ^{R}*Verbum Domini* 33/3 (Jun.1955) 172-175.

118 Map "Succoth under David and Ahab", for YADIN Y., Some Aspects of the Strategy of Ahab and David, *Biblica* 36/3 (Jul.1955) 335.

119 AUER T., *Pharaonen des Buches Exodus* (Regensburg 1951): ^{R}*Biblica* 56/3 (Jul.1955) 372.

120 Explorationes prope "Pinnaculum Templi" et alibi, *Biblica* 36/3 (Jul.1955) 413-6: Olivet Dominus Flevit 413; Jericho, `Ajjul 414; Dura-Europos, Beit-Alpha, Qumran 415.

N° 121 Biblical and Archeological News, *Catholic Biblical Quarterly* 17/3 (Jul.1955) 438-449: Qumran 438; Haifa, Nazareth 440; Negeb, Jericho 121; Ophel, Qumran 332; Saqqâra 443.

122 YEIVIN S., *Milhemet Bar-Kochba* (Jerusalem 1952): [R]*Orientalia* 24/3 (Jul.1955) 340-341.

123 KAUFMANN Y., *The Biblical Account of the Conquest of Palestine* (Jerusalem 1953): [R]*Orientalia* 24/3 (Jul.1955) 340-341.

124 PARROT A., *Le Temple de Jérusalem* (Neuchâtel 1954): [R]*Orientalia* 24/3 (Jul.1955) 341.

125 **Geographia exegetica,** mimeographed Latin lectures on biblical sources (Joshua) of Palestine geography. Rome 1955, Pontifical Biblical Institute. 69 p.
125a   .. Second edition, slightly revised, 1956.

126 MOLIN G., *Die Söhne des Lichtes* (Vienna 1954): [R]*Biblica* 56/4 (Oct.1955) 547-548.

127 MICHEL A., *Le Maître de Justice* (Avignon 1954) : [R]*Biblica* 56/4 (Oct.1955) 548-549.

128 GANSS G., *Saint Ignatius' Idea of a Jesuit University* (Milwaukee 1954): [R]*Gregorianum* 36/4 (Oct.1955) 734-735.

129 WAAGÉ D., *Antioch IV/2 Coins* (Princeton 1952): [R]*Biblica* 56/4 (Oct.1955) 554-555.

130 Current Israel Geography, *Biblica* 37/1 (Jan.1956) 81-98;
                                                        survey:

130a BALDI D., *Enchiridium locorum sacrorum*[2] (Jerusalem 1955) 93.

130b DUNAND M., *De l'Amanus au Sinaï* (Beirut 1953) 95-96.

130c *Encyclopaedia Biblica (Miqra'it II*, Jerusalem 1954) 90-92.

130d *Eretz-Israel Annual II-III* (Jerusalem 1953-4) 87-90.

130e GROLLENBERG L:, *Atlas de la Bible* (Paris 1955) 84-87.

130f GROSVENOR G., ed., *Everyday Life in Ancient Times*[2] (Washington 1953) 96-97.

130g HARLOW V., *The Destroyer of Jesus*[2] (Oklahoma City 1954): 97-98.

130h LEMAIRE P. & BALDI D.., *Atlante storico della Bibbia* (Rome 1955) 81-84.

130i NOTH Martin, *Die Welt des Alten Testaments*[2] (Berlin 1953) 94.

130j VILNAY Z., *Coasts of Israel, etc.* (Tel Aviv 1953) 92.

130k ZIOCK H., *Ägypten-Reiseführer* (Bonn 1955) 92-9.

131 Biblical and Archeological News, *Catholic Biblical Quarterly* 8/1 (Jan.1956) 30-44: Turkey, Antakya 30; Tarsus, Attalia 31; Perga. Antioch-Yalvaç 32; Iconium, Lystra, Derbe 33; Colossae, Ephesus 34; Philadelphia-Alaşehir, Sardis, Boğazköy 35; Beyce-Sultan, Giza 40; Haşor 41; Nazareth, Masada 42; Batâşa, Qumran 43; Bethlehem, Dibon, Tirşa 44.

132 GHIRSHMAN R,, [Susa:] *Village perse-achéménide* (Paris 1954): [R]*Orentalia* 25/1 (Jan.1956) 82-85.

133 INGHOLT H., *Recueil des tessères de Palmyre* (Paris 1955): [R]*Orientalia* 25/1 (Jan.1956) 85.

N⁰ 134 BEHN F., *Ausgrabungen und Ausgräber* (Stuttgart 1955): [R]*Orientalia* 25/1 (Jan.1956) 86.

135 Qumran "Serek a" and Related Fragments, [R]article on BARTHÉLEMY J. & MILIK J., *Discoveries in the Judaean Desert I. Qumran Cave I* (Oxford 1955), in *Orientalia* 25/1 (Jan.1956) 90-99.

136 Date and Unicity of the Exodus, *American Ecclesiastical Review* 134/3 (Mar.1956) 161-182

137 Three Judean Hills in Josue 16,9f, *Biblica* 37/2 (Apr.1956) 209-216.

138 ALIMEN H., *Préhistoire de l'Afrique* (Paris 1955): [R]*Biblica* 27/2 (Apr. 1956) 241-242.

139 NAUMANN Rudolf, *Architektur Kleinasiens* (Tübingen 1955): [R]*Orientalia* 25/2 (Apr.1956) 172-177.

140 WOOLLEY L., *Carchemish III. The Inner Town* (London 1952): [R]*Orientalia* 25/2 (Apr.1956) 178-180.

141 KAPELRUD A., *Ras Sjamra funnene og det Gamle testament* (Oslo 1953): [R]*Orientalia* 25/2 (Apr.1956) 182.

142 BARGUET J. & LECLANT J., *Karnak-Nord IV 1949-1951* (Cairo 1954): [R]*Orientalia* 25/2 (Apr.1956) 195-196.

143 DECAMPS DE MERTZENFELD C., *Inventaire commenté des ivoires phéniciens* (Paris 1954): [R]*Orientalia* 25/2 (Apr.1956) 202-203.

144 LEIPOLDT J., MORENZ S,, *Heilige Schriften* (Leipzig 1955):.. [R]*Orientalia* 25/2 (Apr. 1956) 200-202.

145 LEVENE A., *The Syrian Fathers on Genesis: Mingana Manuscript* (London 1951): [R]*Orientalia* 25/2 (Apr.1956) 202-204.

146   LEWIS Bernard, *Notes and Documents from the Turkish Archives* (Jerusalem 1952) [R]*Orientalia* 25/2 (Apr.1956) 205.

147 ALT A. *Festschrift* (Leipzig 1954): [R]*Verbum Domini* 34/2 (Apr.1956) 102-104.

148 *Hebrew Union College Annual* 25-27 (Cincinnati 1954-6): [R]*Verbum Domini* 25/2(Apr.1956) 114-117.

149 **Guide to Biblical Iran**. Rome 1956, Pontifical Biblical Institute. 168 p.; 14 maps and plans. Lithographed presentation of archeological and religious sites of Persia.

149a ... [R]DU BUIT M.: *Revue Biblique* 64/3 (Jul.1957) 470-471.

149b .. [R]EISSFELDT Otto: *Theologische Literaturzeitung* 82/11 (Nov.1957) 849-850.

149c *New Testament Abstracts*, several items summarized over signature R.N.: vol. 1/3 (1957) 131-2 & 135; vol. 2/1 (1957) 68 & 73-74 & 76 (two); vol. 2/2 (1958) 96 & 169 & 171 & 175; vol. 2/3 (1958) 332b (and others).

*   *   *   *   *

Nº 150   [→ 367 below] **Jerusalem Pontifical Biblical Institute Color-Slide Lectures**: explanatory texts with extensive bibliography to accompany the several slides in 17 sets (in boxes) merchandised by MATSON of Los Angeles: originally 150 slides on "Palestine Holy Places" by Brother Joseph ŠíRA, S.J., 1956; extended to include neighboring Bible-lands on the basis of a nucleus of photos by S. BARTINA S.J. & J.-L. D'ARAGON S.J.:

A   *Archeological Excavations in Palestine*; 1959, 72 p., polycopied: covering three sets, **AS** mostly near Solomonic era; **AN** New Testament era; **AE** varia.

B   *Bethlehem-Judah-Samaria*: 1-59, 24 p., to accompany revised re-edition of one-fourth of Brother ŠíRA's original series (= P below).
B f   French translation of **B** by Père Henri SENÈS S.J.; 1959, 24 p.

C   *Capharnaum-Nazareth*, 1959; 24 p.; for another ¼ of ŠíRA's "**P**".
C f   H. SENÈS, French translation of **C**, 1959; 24 p.

EG   *Egypt*, ¹1958 ¹1959 mimeographed; ³1961, Los Angeles.
EGf   French translation by H. SENÈS of ³1961 revised.

EJ   *East-Jordan*, chiefly <u>Petra</u>, 1959; 24 p.

G   *Greece, the Aegean, Cyprus,*, 1959; 24 p.

H   *Hittite Turkey*, chiefly <u>Boğazköy</u>, 1958. 19 p.
HT   *Hittite-Trojan Turkey* (revisions of **H** noted in catalog **X**).

J *Jerusalem: Sion-Moriah-Olivet*, 1959; 24 p., for another ¼ of ŠÍRA's **"P"** with additions; → **W.**

J f *Jérusalem:* H. SENÈS French translation 1960.

L *Lebanon*, with <u>Damascus</u>, [1]1958.

LSf *Liban et Syrie*, avec <u>Crac, Palmyre</u>; tr. H. SENÈS, [2]1959.

LS *Lebanon-Syria*, [3]1961, 36 p., completely revised; Los Angeles.

M *Mesopotamia*, chiefly <u>Warka</u>, 1958; 13 p.(revisions in catalog **X**).

N *Palestine Sanctuaries*, supplements to ŠÍRA's **P.**

P *Palestine Sanctuaries*, the original set (Nº 150 above), photos all by Brother ŠÍRA and French text by him; English version by F. PEIRCE S.J., 1956.

Q *Qumran*, archeological background of the Dead Sea Scrolls, [1]1958; [2]1959; 24 p.

QM *Qumran* [3]1960. 19 p.; printed; Los Angeles.

QMf H. SENÈS French text 1959; 24 p.

R *Iran*, 1958; 23 p.

S *Sinai*, [1]1958; [2]1959; 24 p.

SN *Sinai, the Land of Gessen and the Exodus*, [3]1960. Matson, Los Angeles. 21 p.; printed.

SNf French of H. SENÈS, 1960; 24 p.

[N° 150] **T** *New Testament Turkey,* ¹1958, 24 p.; ²1959, 32 p.

Tf ²French by H. SENÈS, 1960; 23 p.

TN *New Testament Turkey³.* Los Angeles 1961, Matson. 23 p, printed (revised from mimeographed 32 p., 1960).

W *Jerusalem Way of the Cross,* 1961 (last ¼ of ŠÍRA's **P** with additions). Los Angeles; 16 p. printed (from 1959 mimeo).

Wf French of H. SENÈS 1959.

X *Catalog* of Jerusalem series [→ N° 367 below]. 1000 sites with complete alphabetical cross-index. Los Angeles 1960, Matson Photo Service. 36 p., printed:

> For variant series-and-slide numbering in the subsequent COLORVALD editions, → 367 & 420. Further → 420a **Cumulative index to all slides and bibliographical sources cited in all explanatory booklets**

151 SETTON K., ed., *A History of the Crusades I* (Philadelphia 1955): ᴿ*Biblica* 37/3 (Jul.1956) 373-5.

152 Biblical and Archeological News, *Catholic Biblical Quarterly* 18/3 (Jul.1956) 273-282: Qumran 273; Megiddo 274; Jerusalem, Petra 275;. Halaf, Gordion 276; KaraTepe 278; Kültepe 279; Tulaylât 280; Nimrud, Nippur; Hatra 281.

153 GOODENOUGH Erwin R., *Jewish Symbols in the Greco-Roman Period I-IV* (New York 1953-4): ᴿ*Orientalia* 25/3 (Jul.1956) 310-314.

154 KELSO J. & BARAMKI D., *Excavations at New Testament Jericho* (New Haven 1955): ᴿ*Biblica* 37/4 (Oct.1956) 515-9.

155 DEVAUMAS E., *Liban* (Paris 1954): ᴿ*Biblica* 37/4 (Oct.1956) 520-521.

156 BOULANGER R., *Liban, Guide Bleu* (Paris 1955): [R]*Verbum Domini* 34/5 (Oct.1956) 318-319.

157 AVI-YONAH M. & YEIVIN S., *Qadmoniyyot Arşenu* (The Antiquities of Israel, Tel Aviv 1955): [R]*Christian News from Israel* 7/3 (Dec.1956) 35-37.

158 Il latifondo nella Bibbia, *Civiltà Cattolica* 107,4/6 (Dec.15,1956) 612-619.

159 Homot Yerušalayim le-pî baqîrôt hadašot (The walls of Jerusalem in recent researches), in *Judah and Jerusalem*, Israel Exploration Society 12th Convention, 1956 (Jerusalem 1957) 59-64.

160 WILKEN K., *Biblisches Erleben im Heiligen Land* (Lahr-Dinglingen 1953): [R]*Biblica* 38/1 (Jan.1957) 87-88.

161 UBACH B., *El Sinai: viatge* (Montserrat 1955): [R]*Biblica* 38/1 (Jan. 1957) 88-90.

162 DUSSAUD René, *La pénétration des Arabes en Syrie avant l'Islam* (Paris 1955): [R]*Biblica* 38/1 (Jan.1957) 93-95.

163 Biblical and Archeological News, *Catholic Biblical Quarterly* 19/1 (Jan. 1957) 99-104: Gibeon, Qumran 99; Dibon 100; Jericho, Dothan, Beth-Šᶜʿarim 101; Tel Gath, Haşor 102; Kurnub 103; Mopsuestia, Samira, Tafʿat 104.

N° 164 *Eretz-Israel Annual IV* (Jerusalem 1956): [R]*Verbum Domini* 35/1 (Feb.1957) 48-49.

165 Effossiones Jericho et Dothan 1956, *Biblica* 38/2 (Apr,1957) 226-229.

N° 166 Biblical and Archeological News, *Catholic Biblical Quarterly* 19/2 (Apr. 1957) 234-242: Qumran 234-7 + map; Rujm Island in Dead Sea; Qedron 237; Jericho, Dothan 238; Sinai 239; Eqron-Muqanna 240; Byblos 241.

167 VINCENT L.-Hugues, *Jérusalem de l'Ancien Testament II-III* (Paris 1954): [R]*Orientalia* 26/2 (Apr. 1957) 177-180.

168 GOODENOUGH Erwin R., *Jewish Symbols in the Greco-Roman Period V-V* (New York 1956): [R]*Orientalia* 26/2 (Apr. 1957) 180-1.

169 BRUCK E., *Kirchenväter und soziales Erbrecht* (Berlin 1965): [R]*Verbum Domini* 35/2 (Apr. 1957) 127.

170 MAYANI Z., *Les Hyksos et le monde de la Bible* (Paris 1956): [R]*Vetus Testamentum* 7/2 (Apr. 1957) 219-220.

171 Biblical and Archeological News, *Catholic Biblical Quarterly* 19/3 (Jul. 1957) 359-360: Qumran, Jericho.

172 MOSCATI S., *I predecessori d'Israele* (Rome 1956): [R]*Journal of Semitic Studies* 1/3 (Jul. 1957) 267-8.

173 Status of the Warka Excavation, *Orientalia* 26/3 (Jul. 1957) 185-256.

173a ... summary by PARROT A., *Syria* 36 (1959) 141-142.

174 ORLINSKY Harry M., *Ancient Israel* (New York 1954): [R]*Orientalia* 26/3 (Jul. 1957) 288.

175 ROSÉN H., *Ha-'Ibrit še-lanu* (Our Hebrew Language in the Light of Linguistics, Tel Aviv 1955): [R]*Orientalia* 26/3 (Jul. 1957) 288-291.

176 Biblical and Archeological News, *Catholic Biblical Quarterly* 19/4 (Oct. 1957) 489-492: Pella in Macedon 389; Calvary 490; Jîb, Balata, Qasila 491; Qumran, Lebanon 392.

177 GOITEIN S., *Jews and Arabs: their contacts through the ages* (New York 1955): [R]*Orientalia* 26/4 (Oct.1957) 387-388.

178 ALINE DE SION sœur, *La Forteresse Antonia* (Paris 1955): [R]*Verbum Domini* 35/6 (Dec.1957) 367-369.

179 Bethlehem today, *Jesuit Blackrobe* (Dec.1957) 3-7.

180 Contributions to *Lexikon für Theologie und Kirche*[2]. ed. HOFER J. & RAHNER K., (Freiburg im Breisgau 1957-, Herder): Abilene, Akko, Apameia, Arwad, Baalbek vol. 1 (1957) 44 & 238-9 & 684 & 812. – Bether, Beth Jeschimoth, Byblos, Chazael: 2 (1958) 810 & 840 & 847 & 1242. – Dor, Duma, Ephraim: 3 (1959) 518-9 & 598 & 923-6. – Gath, Gaza, Gezer, Haifa: 4 (1960) 528-9 & 534-5 & 878-9 & 1324. – Havvot Jair, Hebron, Herodeion, Jabesch, Jaffa, Jebus(im), Jobeljahr, Jutta, Karnaim 5 (1961) 40 & 51 & 262-3 & 829 & 851-2 & 887 & 979-980 & 1230 & 1372, – Kirjath Jearim Lachish, Maiuma, Malsteine: 6 (1961) 306-7 & 752 & 1307 & 1335. – Negeb, Oronaim, oss(u)ar(ium): 7 (1962) 865 & 1237 & 1270 - Rages, Rimmon, ROBINSON E.: 8 (1963) 971 & 1314 & 1344. - ROPES J.; Sabbatjahr, Salton, Seboim, Sikelag, Teleilat Ghassul: 9 (1964) 39 & 192 & 278 & 559 & 752 & 1343-4. -- Thimna 10 (1970) 115

181 "Kittim" War or "Sectaries'" Liturgy?, review art. on. Y. YADIN, *Megillat milhemet Benê-Or* (The war of the Sons of Light, Jerusalem 1957) in *Biblica* 39/1 (Jan.1958) 84-93.

182 (→242) HOFER J, RAHNER K., ed., *Lexikon für Theologie und Kirche*[2] *I* (Freiburg 1957): [R]*Biblische Zeitschrift* 3/1 (Jan.1958) 139-141.

183 GOLDMAN Hetty, *Excavations at Gözlü Küle, Tarsus II* (Princeton 1956): [R]*Orientalia* 27/1 (Jan.1958) 125-127.

184 GRAPOW H Fest., *Ägyptologische Studien* (Berlin 1955): [R]*Verbum Domini* 36/1 (Feb.1958) 55-56.

185 EISSFELDT O., *Einleitung in das Alte Testament²* (Tübingen 1956): [R]*Biblica* 39/2 (Apr.1958) 231-2.

186 BLINZLER J., *Der Prozess Jesu²* (Regensburg 1955): [R]*Biblica* 39/2 (Apr.1958) 242-243.

187 GROLLENBERG L, *Atlas of the Bible* (→ 136; tr. London 1956): [R]*Biblica* 39/2 (Apr.1958) 243-244.

188 KRAELING Carl, *Dura-Europos: the Synagogue* (Glückstadt 1956): [R]*Biblica* 39/2 (Apr.1958) 255-264.

189 Biblical and Archeological News, *Catholic Biblical Quarterly* 20/2 (Apr.1958). 218-224: Bethlehem 218, Beth-Zur, Jericho, Qumran 219, Balâta 220, ˈAmman, Gath, Kabara, Meşer 221, Mellaha, Šabe Şion 222, Jerusalem 223.

190 *Emcyclopaedia (miqra'ît) Biblica III* (Jerusalem 1950): [R]*Christian News from Israel* 9/1 (Jun.1958) 43-45.

191 CASTELLINO G., *Libro dei Salmi* (Torino 1955): [R]*Verbum Domini* 36/3 (Jun.1958) 179-181.

192 KISSANE Edward J., *The Book of Psalms* (Dublin 1954): [R]*Verbum Domini* 36/3 (Jun.1958) 179-181.

193 GALLING Kurt, ed., *Die Religion in Geschichte und Gegenwart³* I (Tübingen 1957),
                II (1958),
                III (1959): [R]*Verbum Domini* 36/3 (Jun.1958) 184-6; 37/5 (Oct.1959) 316-7; 39/4 (Aug.1961) 226-7.

194 HAHN Herbert F., *The Old Testament in Modern Research* (Philadelphia 1954): [R]*Verbum Domini* 36/3 (Jun.1958) 186-7.

195 MADER E., *Mambre* (Freiburg 1957): [R]*Biblische Zeitschrift* 2/2 (Jul.1958) 315-318.

196 Biblical and Archeological News, *Catholic Biblical Quarterly* 20/3 (Jul. 1958) 354-359: Perga 354; Boğazköy, Ras Shamra, Qumran 355; Dothan, Azor, Caesarea, Ascalon 357.

197 Scavi e pellegrinaggi in Terra Santa, *Civiltà Cattolica* 109,3/1 (Jul 1,1958) 52-66: Qumran 53; Tirṣa, Dotan, Bet-Ṣur, Balâta 54; Jîb 55; Jericho 56; Nazareth 62 64; Haṣor, Bet-Šᵉ`arim 62; Beersheba, Meṣer 63; Caesarea, Kerak, Gath 64.

198 RICE F. & SAID M., *Jerusalem Arabic* (mimeographed, Washington 1953): [R]*Orientalia* 27/3 (Jul.1958) 317-9 [24 (1965) .. *Eastern Arabic* (printed 1960)].

199 Les murs de Jéricho, *Bible et Terre Sainte* 14 (Oct.1968) 10-17.

200 AHARONI Y., *Hitnaḥalut šibtê Yiśra'el bᵃ-Galîl ha-Elyon* (Occupation of Upper Galilee by the Tribes of Israel, Jerusalem 1957): [R]*Biblica* 39/4 (Oct.1958) 506-507.

201 *Yehudâ wi-Yrušalayim* (→ N° 159, Jerusalem 1956/7): [R]*Biblica* 39/4 (Oct.1958) 515.

202 BARNETT R.D., *Catalogue of the Nimrud Ivories* (London 1957): [R]*Biblica* 39/4 (Oct.1958) 516-518.

203 QUASTEN J., *Patrology I-II* (Utrecht 1949-1953): [R]*Biblica* 39/4 (Oct.1958) 519-521.

204 Biblical and Archeological News, *Catholic Biblical Quarterly* 20/4 (Oct.1958) 507-512: <u>Sinai</u>, <u>Ras-Shamra</u> 507; <u>Jerusalem</u>, East-Jordan <u>Pella</u> 508; <u>Petra</u>, `Amman 509; <u>Azor</u>, <u>Sahne</u> 510; <u>Haşor</u>, <u>Hanita</u> 511; <u>Shanidar</u>..

205 WETZEL F., *Babylon der Spätzeit* (Berlin 1957): [R]*Orientalia* 27/4 (Oct.1954) 451-452.

206 TEDESCHE S., *First Maccabees* (New York 1950), *Second* (1954); HADAS H., *Third-Fourth* (1953); *Aristeas* (1951), in Dropsie College Jewish Apocryphal Literature: [R]*Verbum Domini* 36/5 (Oct.1958) 307-309.

207 DÍAZ Jesús, *Enquiridion Bíblico Bilingüe* (Segovia 1954): [R]*Verbum Domini* 36/5 (Oct.1958) 312-313.

208 JEREMIAS J. & ADOLPH K., *Rabbinischer Index zu* STRACK-BILLERBECK (Munich 1956): [R]*Verbum Domini* 36/5 (Oct.1958) 318.

209 **Jordan Sites of Priests'-Tour,** 1958. 48 p., mimeographed; índex.

210 Biblical and Archeological News, *Catholic Biblical Quarterly* 21/1 (Jan.1959) 55-59; <u>Sardis</u>, <u>Haşor</u> 55; <u>Carmel</u> San Brocardo 58.

211 DE VAUX R., *Institutions de l'Ancien Testament I-II* (Paris 1958-1960): [R]*Orientalia* 28/1 (Jan.1959) 109-110 ....

212 DU BUIT M., *Géographie de la Terre Sainte* (Paris 1958): [R]*Orientalia* 28/1 (Jan 1959) 110.

213 MACH R., *Der Zaddik in Talmud und Midrasch* (Leiden 1957): [R]*Orientalia* 28/1 (Jan.1959) 108-109.

214 Planning to Visit the Holy Land?, *Homiletic and Pastoral Review* 59/5 (Feb.1959) 430-434.

215 RENGSTORF K., *Rabbinische Texte* (Stuttgart 1945): [R]*Verbum Domini* 37/1 (Feb.1959) 49-51.

216 [BEN-OR J.L.], Advent Lectures at the Pontifical Institute in Jerusalem, *Christian News from Israel* 8 (1959) 18.

217 SNAITH N., *The Jews from Cyrus to Herod* (Wellington 1956): [R]*Bibliotheca Orientalis* 16/3 (May 1959) 154-155.

218 ETTELDORF R., *The Catholic Church in the Middle East* (New York 1959): [R]*Homiletic and Pastoral Review* 59/9 (Jun.1959) 870-874.

219 "Ghassulian" in Palestine Chronological Nomenclature, in *Analecta Biblica* 10 = *Studia Biblica* et *Orientalia* (Festschrift P.I.B. anni 50) vol.1. VT (Rome 1959 407-421 =) *Biblica* 40/2 (Apr.1959) 541-555.

220 Report from Palestine, *Catholic Biblical Quarterly* 21/2 (Jul.1959) 341-5: Nazareth, Gath, Jaffa 341; Qumran 342; Calvary 343; Adlun 344.

221 VRIEZEN T,, *Outline of Old Testament Theology* (Wageningen 1958): [R]*Orientalia* 28/3 (Jul.1959) 317-320.

222 Report from Palestine, *Catholic Biblical Quarterly* 21/4 (Oct.1959) 491-495: Jerusalem, Jib, Caesarea, Minya 491; Bet-Šan, Nazareth, Sepphoris 492; Cairo 493; Chenoboskion, Sulayb, Buhayn 494.

223 GLUECK Nelson, *Rivers in the Desert* (New York 1959): [R]*Christian News from Israel* 10/3 (Dec. 1959) 39-42.

224 Ap(h)eq(a) and ʿAzeqa, *Biblica* 41/1 (Jan.1960) 41-63.

225 JIRKU Anton, *Die Welt der Bibel* (Stuttgart 1957): [R]*Biblica* 41/1 (Jan.1960) 85-86.

226 Report from Palestine, *Catholic Biblical Quarterly* 22/1 (Jan.1960) 76-84: Makmiš, Jerusalem 76; Olduvai, Buhen 79; Antakya, Izmir, Boğazköy, Konya, Kayseri 81; Troy, Sardis 82; Gordion, Philippi, Amphipolis, Salonike, Beroea 83.

227 PIRENNE Jacqueline, *À la découverte de l'Arabie* (Paris 1958): [R]*Orientalia* 29/1 (Jan.1960) 117-120.

N° 228 **Programma delle escursioni Giudea-Galilea.** Jerusalem 1960, Pontificio Istituto Biblico. 120 pp. in two booklets; maps,indices.

229 [POTIN Jean], Teleilat Ghassul: le P. North exhume une nouvelle civilisation, *Bible et Terre Sainte* 28 (Apr.1960) 19.

230 Report from Palestine, *Catholic Biblical Quarterly* 22/2 (Apr.1960) 192-196: Ghassul 192; Jericho, Deir'Alla, Lisan 195.

231 BEHLER G., *Les Confessions de Jérémie* (Tournai 1959): [R]*Verbum Domini* 38/2 (Apr.1960) 128.

232 VOEGELIN Eric, *Order and History I. Israel and Revelation* (Oxford 1956): [R]*Bibliotheca Orientalis* 18/1 (May 1960) 85-87.

233 DEVESCOVI U., *L'Alleanza nell'esateuco* (Macao 1957): [R]*Biblica* 41/3 (Jul.1960) 301-303.

234 COSTIGAN Michael E., [North's] Magic Carpet to the Near East, *Homiletic and Pastoral Review* 60/10 (Jul.1960) 895-901.

235 VANDEN BERGHE L., *Archéologie de l'Iran ancien* (Leiden 1959): [R]*Orientalia* 23/3 (Jul.1960) 339-342.

236 Teleilat Ghassul: communication, *Revue Biblique* 67/3 (Jul.1960) 368-370.

237 A Unique New Palestine Art-Form, *Estudios Eclesiásticos* 34/134 (Jul. 1960) 381-390 = A. FERNÁNDEZ Festschrift 77-86.

237a PRITCHARD James B., *Hebrew Inscriptions and Stamps from Gibeon* (Philadelphia 1959): [R]*Catholic Biblical Quarterly* 22/3 (Jul.1960) 361f.

237b   .. another appraisal in *Biblica* 41,4 (Oct. 1960) 443.

238 Report from Palestine, *Catholic Biblical Quarterly* 22/3 (Jul.1960) 317-323: Qumran 238; Akzib,Carmel 238; Cenacle, Nazareth 319; Abu-Gosh 320; Abu Simbel 321; Gordion 322; Gaziantep 323.

239 **Archeology and Christian Origins**, St. Louis University mimeographed syllabus booklet, 1960. 32 p.

240 KALLAI Z., *Northern Boundaries of Judah* (Jerusalem 1960): [R]*Biblica* 41/4 (Oct.1960) 425-426.

241 Report from Palestine, *Catholic Biblical Quarterly* 22/4 (Oct.1960) 422-429: Qumran, Balāṭa, Jîb 422; Capharnaum, Yabne, `En-Gedi, Bet-šan 423; Caesarea-M, Garizim 424; Machaerus, Hebron, Sodom, Palmyra; 426 Mari, Dura-Europos 426; Halaf, Allun, Palmyra, Huwayra 427; Ladiqiya, Apameia-Mudîq 428.

242 *Lexikon für Theologie und Kirche*[2] [→ N° 182] II-III (Freiburg 1959): [R]*Biblische Zeitschrift* 4/2 (Jul.1960) 312-4.

243 Realizzazioni intorno a Bêt-Scian, *Bibbia e Oriente* 3/1(Jan.1961) 22.

244 Excavations of last Christmas in the Holy Land, *Jesuit Bulletin* 39/6 (Dec.1960) 8-9.

245 BOEHRINGER Erich ed., *Neue deutsche Ausgrabungen im Mittelmeergebiet* (Berlin 1959): [R]*Orientalia* 30/2 (Apr.1961) 229-231.

246 Scavi palestinesi sotto bandiera pontificia, *Bibbia e Oriente* 3/3 (May 1961) 86-89.

247 ALBRIGHT W.F. Festschrift, *The Bible and the Ancient Near East*, ed. G.Ernest WRIGHT (Garden City NY 1961): [R]*Catholic Biblical Quarterly* 23/4 (Oct.1961) 465-468.

N° 248 *Conference of Christian Doctrine Holy Bible IV. Isaia to Malachi* (Paterson 1961): [R]*Catholic Book Reporter* 1/5 (Oct.1961) 13-14.

249 **Ghassul 1960 Excavation Report**: Analecta Biblica 14. Rome 1961, Pontifical Biblical Institute. xiii-88 p.; 19 fig.; xxiii pl.

   Scholarly reviews:
249a NOTH M., [R]*Zeitschrift des deutschen Palästina-Vereins* 78/2 (1962) 190-191.

249b WRIGHT G. Ernest, [R]*Catholic Biblical Quarterly* 25/2 (Apr. 1963) 202-304.

249c PERROT J., [R]*Orientalia* 32/1 (Jan.1963) 140-147.

249d DE VAUX R., [R]*Revue Biblique* 70 (1963) 626-627.

249e FOHRER G., [R]*Zeitschrift für die alttestamentliche Wissenschaft* 74/3 (1962) 353.

249f [62d General Meeting AIA:] [R]*American Journal of Archaeology* 65/2 (Apr.1961) 191.

249g BAGATTI B., [R]*La Terra Santa* 38 (1962) 96.

250 SINT Josef, *Pseudonymität im Altertum* (Innsbruck 1960): [R]*Theological Studies* 22/4 (Oct.1961) 706.

251 **Prophetism as a Philosophy of History:** 24 OT lectures at St.Louis University theologate, St. Marys,Kansas, 1961. 56 p., mimeographed.

252 STÉVE M.-J., *The Living World of the Bible* (New York 1961) [R]*Catholic Book Reporter* 1/6 (Dec.1961) 16.

253 **College-Level Christianity;** lectures on revelation and infallibility Milwaukee 1962, Marquette University. 80 p.

253a .. reedited as **The Christ of the Gospels,** 1965.

254 DE VAUX R., *Ancient Israel, its Life and Institutions* (→ Nº.211) tr., New York 1961): [R]*America* 106/18 (Feb.10,1962) 630.

255 CARMIGNAC J. & GUILBERT P., *Textes de Qumran I* (Paris 1961): [R]*Catholic Biblical Quarterly* 24/1 (Jan.1962) 101-2.

256 KINGSTON F., *French Existentialism* (Toronto 1961): [R]*Catholic Book Reporter* 2/1 (Mar.1962) 30-31.

257 Scripture and Secularization, *America* 106 (Mar.10,1962) 757-760.

257a .. CONWAY J., comment, *St.Louis Review* (Nov 2,1962) 24.

258 Holy Thursday or Holy Tuesday ?, *St.Joseph's Magazine* 63/4 (Apr.1962) 14-15 + 45.

259 Chenoboskion and Q ["Quelle", assumed Mk-Lk-Mt source], *Catholic Biblical Quarterly* 24/2 (Apr. 1962) 154-170.

260 REHRL S., *Das Problem der Demut im .. NT* (Münster 1961): [R]*Theological Studies* 23/2 (Apr.1962) 345-6.

261 LAPP Paul, *Palestinian Ceramic Chronology 200 B.C. - A.D. 70* (New Haven 1961): [R]*Catholic Biblical Quarterly* 24/3 (July 1962) 309-313.

262 CORNFELD G., *Adam to Daniel* (New York 1961): [R]*Manuscripta* 6 (Oct.1962) 168-9.

N° 263 TESTA E., *Il simbolismo dei Giudeo-Cristiani* (Jerusalem 1962): [R]*Catholic Biblical Quarterly* 24/4 (Oct.1962) 441-3.

264 VINK J., *Leviticus* (Roermond 1962): [R]*Catholic Biblical Quarterly* 24/4 (Oct.1962) 449-451.

265 The Genetic Image of God, *Spiritual Life* 8/4 (Winter 1962) 224-233.

266 The Qumran Reservoirs, in M. GRUENTHANER memorial *The Bible in Current Catholic Thought*, ed.J. MCKENZIE (St.Marys Theological Studies 1; New York 1962, Herder & H.) 100-132.

266a ... noted in ROHRHIRSCH : F., Katholische Universität Eichstätt *Qumran-Projekt* 2001.

267 Le camp de Josué autour de Ghassul, *Bible et Terre Sainte* 52 (Jan.1963) 6-21.

268 TOCCI F., *La Siria nell'età di Mari* (Rome 1960): [R]*Orientalia* 32/1 (Jan.1963) 107-109.

269 VAN ZYL A., *The Moabites* (Leiden 1960): [R]*Orientalia* 32/1 (Jan.1963) 107-9.

269a DANIEL-ROPS H., *Daily Life in the Times of Jesus* (New York 1963): [R]*Catholic Book Reporter* 2/3 (Mar.1963) 27.

270 THOMPSON J., *The Bible and Archaeology* (Grand Rapids 1962): [R]*Catholic Biblical Quarterly* 25/2 (Apr.1963) 223-224.

271 **The Book of Psalms, parts 3 and 4 with commentary:** Paulist Pamphlet Bible Series, 45 & 46. New York 1964, Paulist. 96 & 80 p.

272 A Frontier Jerome: GRUENTHANER, *American Ecclesiastical Review* 148/5 (May 1963) 289-304; 148/6 (Jun,1963) 388-411; 149/1 (Jul.1963) 41-50.

273 DOWNEY G., *Ancient Antioch* (Princeton 1963): [R]*Journal of Biblical Literature* 82/2 (Apr.1963) 228-9.

274 Archeology and Catholic Bible Study, *Australasian Catholic Record* 40/3 (Jul.1963) 243-248.

275 Negro Segregation in America, *Twentieth Century Australian Quarterly* 18/3 (Summer 1963) 116-127.

276 BRAIDWOOD R. & HOWE B., *Prehistoric Investigations in Iraqi Kurdistan* (Chicago 1960): [R]*Orientalia* 32/3 (Jul.1963) 344-347.

277 McEWAN C., *Soundings at Tell Fakhariyah* (Chicago 1958): [R]*Orientalia* 32/3 (Jul.1963) 347-8.

278 Brother Antonio VIVES S.J., *Biblica* 44/3 (Jul.1963) 396-7.

279 KOPP C., *The Holy Places of the Gospels* (New York 1963): [R]*Theological Studies* 24/3 (Sep.1963) 526.

280 HORN E., *Ichnographia Terrae Sanctae* (Jerusalem 1962): [R]*Catholic Biblical Quarterly* 25/4 (Oct.1963) 369-381.

281 Theology of the Chronicler, *Journal of Biblical Literature* 82/4 (Oct.1963) 369-381.

281a .. on which [ABRAMSKY S.], Teologia b[e]-seper Dibrê ha-Yamîm [Book of Chronicles], *Beth Mikra* 9/3 (1964) 204-209.

282 TEILHARD and the Many Adams, *Continuum* 1/3 (Autumn 1963) 329-342.

N° 283 TEILHARD and the Problem of Creation, *Theological Studies* 24/4 (Dec.1963) 577-601.

284 ORLINSKY H., ed., *The Torah; the Five Books of Moses* (Philadelphia 1963): [R] *Theological Studies* 24/4 (Dec.1963) 713-714.

285 **A Catholic Path through PRITCHARD's ANET.** Milwaukee 1964, Marquette University. 16 p., mimeographed.

286 LAMBERT W., *Babylonian Wisdom Literature* (Oxford 1960): [R]*Orientalia* 33/1 (Jan.1964) 103-105.

287 DRUBBEL A., *Numeri* (Roermond 1963): [R]*Catholic Biblical Quarterly* 26/2 (Apr.1964) 262-3.

288 The American Scripture Century, *American Ecclesiastical Review* 150/5 (May 1964) 314-345: dense survey.

289 [-295, numbering slightly changed from earlier editions of this bibliography:] **Israel's Chronicle** (the third OT history). St Marys KS 1963, St.Louis University theologate. x-423 p. (5 vol.), mimeographed.

290 [materials and formulation for] VAN ACKEREN Gerald, Is All Revelation in Scripture?, *Proceedings of the Catholic Theological Society of America* 17 (1962) 249-261.

291 HEIDER L.J. (obituary), Missouri-Wisconsin *Province News-Letter* 23/7 (Apr.1964) 142-144.

292 Form-Criticism: the New Testament, (Melbourne Univ.) *Prospect* 7/1 (1964) 4-7.

293 Ghassul's New-Found Jar Incision, *Annual of the Department of Antiquities of Jordan* 8-9 (1964) 68-78.

294 *Encyclopaedia Biblica (miqra'ît)* IV (Jerusalem 1962): [R]*Orientalia* 33/2 (Apr.1964) 299-230.

N° 295 POELMAN Roger, *Times of Grace: the Sign of Forty in the Bible*, [R]*Woodstock Letters* 93/2 (Apr.1964) 225-6.

296 DE FRAINE Jean, *Genesis* (Roermond 1963): [R]*Catholic Biblical Quarterly* 26/3 (Jul.1964) 366-7.

297 MOSCATI S., *Historical Art in the Ancient Near East* (Rome 1963): [R]*Catholic Biblical Quarterly* 26/3 (Jul.1964) 381.

298 The Cain Music, *Journal of Biblical Literature* 83/4 (Dec.1964) 373-398.

299 The Scope of Infallibility, *Continuum* 2/4 (Jan.1965) 555-574.

299a .. cited in *Life* 69/25 (Dec.17,1965) 20.

299b .. in *Herder-Korrespondenz* 19/9 (Jun.1965) 438

300 HORAIN C.M., *L'identité des lieux de la Galilée* (Gand 1963): [R]*Journal of Biblical Literature* 84/1 (Mar.1965) 98.

301 Leviticus, *Encyclopedia Britannica* (Chicago 1965) 13,1004-6.

302 In *Enciclopedia de la Biblia* (Garriga: Barcelona):302a Anatolia, vol.1 (1963) 472-483; 302b Ghassul, 3 (1964) 717-9; 302c Jericó, 4 (1964) 334-340; 302d Jubileo, 4 (1964) 710-711; 382e Sociología bíblica, 6 (1965) 773-778.

303 In *Catholic Encyclopedia for School and Home* (New York 1966, McGraw-Hill; not = 384): 303a Byblos vol.2, 146; 303b Calvary 2,169; 303c Carchemish 2,272-3; 303d Jericho 5,652-3; 303e Jerusalem 5,655-7; 303f Red Sea 9,185-6; 303g Sinai 10,104-5.

304 LUCAS A., [4]HARRIS J., *Ancient Egyptian Materials* (London 1962): [R]*Orientalia* 34/1 (1965) 87-89.

N⁰ 305 FINEGAN Jack, *Handbook of Biblical Chronology* (Princeton 1964): *Catholic Biblical Quarterly* 27/1 (Jan. 1965) 59-61.

306 SALLER Sylvester, *Excavations of Dominus Flevit II. The Jebusite Burial Place* (Jerusalem 1964): ᴿ*Catholic Biblical Quarterly* 27/2 (Jan. 1965) 76-78.

307 Keeping Up-to-Date on Biblical Exegesis, *The Bible Today* 16 (Feb.1965) 1061-6.

308 **Geobiblica**, lectiones de geographia biblica. Rome 1965, Pontificio Istituto Biblico. 56 p.

309 LANCELLOTTI Angelo, *Sintassi ebraica nel greco dell'Apocalissi I* (Assisi 1964): ᴿ*Journal of Biblical Literature* 84/1 (Mar. 1965) 98.

310 ORTHMAN Winfried, *Frühe Keramik von Boğazköy* (Berlin 1963): ᴿ*Orientalia* 34/3 (Apr.1965) 478-482.

311 FISCHER Franz, *Die hethitische Keramik von Boğazköy* (Berlin 1963): ᴿ*Orientalia* 34/3 (Apr.1965) also 478-482.

312 LOHFINK Norbert, *Das Siegeslied am Schilfmeer* (Frankfurt 1965): ᴿ*Biblica* 46/3 Apr.1965) 386-7 [qualified in N° 362 #3].

313 YADIN Yigael, *Scroll of the War of the Sons of Light* (N° 181 tr.: London 1962): ᴿ*Biblica* 46/2 (Apr.1965) 387-8.

314 Scripture Trends in 1964, *American Ecclesiastical Review* 152/6 (June 1965) 361-397.

314a ..   noted in ROSŁON Józef, *Roczniki Teologiczne-Kanoniczne*.

315 MAYER L. Festschrift, *Eretz Israel* 7 (1964): ᴿ*Biblica* 46/3 (Jul. 1965) 480-481.

316 PRITCHARD James B., *The Bronze Age Cemetery at Gibeon* (Philadelphia 1963): [R]*Biblica* 46/3 (Jul.1965) 389-390.

317 DE FRAINE J., *Esdras en Nehemias* (Roermond 1981): [R]*Biblica* 46/3 (Jul.1965) 393.

318 Some Links between the Hurrians and the Language of the Exodus, in H. BOSSERT memorial, *Jahrbuch für kleinasiatische Forschung* 2/1 (1965) 343-357.

319 WINNETT Fred & REED William, *Excavations at Dibon:* Annual ASOR 37 (New Haven 1964): [R]*Biblica* 46/3 (Jul.1965) 464-465.

320 AMIRAN Ruth, *Ancient Pottery of Eretz Israel* (Jerusalem 1963): [R]*Biblica* 46/3 (Jul.1965) 486-488.

321 GIEDION S., *The Eternal Present II. The Beginnings of Architecture* (London 1964): [R]*Orientalia* 35/1 (Jan.1966) 65-69.

322 LEZINE A., *Mahdiya [Tunis]* (Paris 1965): [R]*Orientalia* 35/1 (Jan. 1966) 75.

323 **Modern Catholic Bible Study**, in English and Korean. Seoul Feb.14-18, 1966. 32 p.

324 [MOSCATI S.,] *Missione archeologica italiana a Malta* (Rome 1964): [R]*Orientalia* 35/2 (Apr.1966) 195-200.

325 GOODENOUGH E., *Jewish Symbols in the Greco-Roman Period* (N° 153 & 168 above), vol.9-11 (New York 1964): [R]*Orientalia* 35/2 (Apr.1966) 201-203.

326 CASAL Jean-Marie, *Fouilles d'Amri [Pakistan]* (Paris 1964): [R]*Orientalia* 35.2 (Apr.1966) 204.

N° 327 CORNFELD G., *Pictorial Biblical Encyclopedia* (New York 1964): [R]*Interpretation* 20/2 (Apr.1966) 238-242.

328 Old Testament Horizon of 1966, *American Ecclesiastical Review* 154/6 (Jun.1966) 361-383.

329 New Testament Horizon of 1966, *AER* 155/1 (Jul.1966) 33-52.

330 Caleb, *Bibbia e Oriente* 6 (G. RINALDI Festschrift) 167-171.

331 HYATT J. Philip, *The Heritage of Biblical Faith* (St.Louis 1964): [R]*Biblica* 47/3 (Jul.1969) 475-6.

332 In memoriam Jean DE FRAINE S.J., *Catholic Biblical Quarterly* 28/4 (Oct. 1966) 480.

333 DE FRAINE J., *Adam and the Family of Man* (New York 1965): [R]*Catholic Biblical Quarterly* 28/4 (Oct.1966) 498-499.

334 MYERS John M., *First Chronicles, Second Chronicles, Ezra-Nehemiah*: Anchor Bible 12,13,14 (Garden City NY 1965): [R]*Catholic Biblical Quarterly* 28/4 (Oct.1966) 519-524.

335 BECKMANN Johannes, *Die heilige Schrift in den katholischen Missionen* (Schöneck 1966): [R]*Catholic Biblical Quarterly* 29/1 (Jan. 1967) 129-132.

336 **Teilhard and the Creation of the Soul**, with an introduction by Karl RAHNER. Milwaukee 1967, Bruce. ➜ 282 283 337a,b 374.

336a .. [R]WRIGHT J.H., *Theological Studies* 29,1 (Mar.1968) 139-140

337a Genesis and Teilhard, Catholic Biblical Association 1962 Maryknoll meeting ¬ *Catholic Biblical Quarterly* 24/4 (Oct.1962) 426.

337b Proof-Texts for the Creation of Souls, CBA 1964 Flushing meeting ¬ *CBQ* 26/4 (1964) 469.

338a The Trauma of King Saul, *The Bible Today* 29 (Mar.1967) 2048-2059 (-2061).

338b   VAN SETERS John, *The Hyksos* (New Haven 1966): [R]*Orientalia* 36/2 (Apr.1967) 255-257.

339   GOODENOUGH E., *Jewish Symbols* (→ N° 153, 168, 203) 12 (New York 1966): [R]*Orientalia* 36/2 (Apr.1967) 258-259.

340   MELLINK M., ed., *Dark Ages and Nomads [Iran]* (Istanbul 1964): [R]*Orientalia* 36/2 (Apr.1967) 262-263.

341   THIELE Erwin R., *The Mysterious Numbers of the Hebrew Kings*[2] (Grand Rapids 1965): [R]*Catholic Biblical Quarterly* 29/2 (Apr. 1967) 181-183.

342   RANDELLINI Lino, *Il libro delle Cronache* (Rome 1966): [R]*Biblica* 48/2 (Apr.1967) 311-312.

343 **Chronistae opus is sua scaena postexsilica.** Roma 1967, Pontificio Istituto Biblico. 64 p.
                              Incorporating:

343a   Universalismo y segregación postexílica, Congreso Bíblico, Madrid 1965 → N° 411 below.

343b   *Universalismus adversus particularismum in nascente Judaismo postbiblico.* Barcelona San Cugat 1967.

343c **Historiae salutis cur tertium compendium biblicum**? Rome c.1967.

344   <u>Ophir/Parvaim</u> and <u>Petra/Joktheel</u>, 1965 *Fourth World Congress of Jewish Studies* (Jerusalem 1967) 1,197-201.

345 The Trilemma of David's Rise, 1965 *Geneva Old Testament Congress* [J? E? P? noted in N° 375 below].

N° 346   PRITCHARD J.B., *Winery, Defenses, and Soundings at Gibeon* (Philadelphis 1964): [R]*Biblica* 48/3 (Jul.1967) 325.

347   CAMPBELL Edward F., *Chronology of the Amarna Letters* (Baltimore 1964): [R]*Orientalia* 36/3 (Jul.1967) 325.

348   HOEPFNER Wolfram, *Forschungen an der Nordküste Kleinasiens I. Herakleia* (Vienna 1966): [R]*Orientalia* 36/3 (July 1967) 372-3.

349   LANGLOTZ Ernst, *Die kulturelle und künstlerische Hellenisierung .. durch Phokaia* (Cologne 1966): [R]*Orientalia* 36/3 (Jul.1967) 387.

350 Separated Spiritual Substances in the Old Testament [angels], *Catholic Biblical Quarterly* 29/3 (L. HARTMAN Festschrift, Jul.1967) 419-442 = 113-143.

351   AHARONI Yohanan, *The Land of the Bible, a Historical Geography* (London 1966): [R]*Biblica* 48/3 (Jul.1967) 452-456.

352   KENYON Kathleen M., *Amorites and Canaanites* (1963 Schweich Lectures; London 1966): [R]*Biblica* 48/3 (Jul.1967) 456-458.

353   VOGT R., *Studie zur nachexilischen Gemeinde in Esra-Nehemia* (Werl 1966): [R]*Biblica* 48/3 (Jul.1967) 469.

354   NAGEL Wolfram, *Djamdat Nasr-Kulturen und frühdynastische Buntkeramiker* (Berlin 1964): [R]*Orientalia* 36/4 (Oct.1967) 462-464.

355 HROUDA Barthel, *Kulturgeschichte des assyrischen Flachbildes* (Bonn 1965): [R]*Orientalia* 36/4 (Oct.1967) 478-9.

356 FREYER-SCHAUENBERG Birgitte, *Elfenbeine aus dem samischen Heraion* (Hamburg 1966): [R]*Orientalia* 37/2 (Apr.1968) 255.

357 MONTAGNINI Felice, *Il libro di Isaia, parte prima* (Brescia 1966) [R]*Verbum Domini* 45 (1967) 243-244.

358 MICHAELI Frank, *Les livres des Chroniques, d'Esdras et de Néhémie*
(Neuchâtel 1967): ^R*Biblica* 48/4 (Oct.1967) 640-642.

359 SUKENIK E. volume, *Eretz-Israel* 8 (1967): ^R*Biblica* 48/4 (Oct.1967)
641-642.

360 DOTHAN Trude, *The Philistines and their Material Culture* (in
Hebrew; Jerusalem 1967): ^R*Biblica* 48/4 (Oct.1967) 645-647.

361 RAPAPORT U., *History of Israel in the Period of the Second Temple* (in
Hebrew; Jerusalem 1967): ^R*Biblica* 48/4 (Oct.1967) 647-649.

362 LIVER J. ed., *The Military History of the Land of Israel in Biblical
Times* (in Hebrew; Tel Aviv 1965): ^R*Biblica* 48/4 (Oct.1967) 647-649.

363 HACHMANN R. & KUSCHKE A., *Bericht über Kamid el-Loz (Liba-
non)* (Bonn 1966): ^R*Biblica* (Oct.1967) 653.

364 In *New Catholic Encyclopedia* (New York 1967, McGraw-Hill; see
also N° 303):
364a Byblos, vol. 2, p. 918-9;
364b Jubilee, vol. 7, p. 1141.
364c Palmyra, vol. 10, p. 936.
364d ROOTHAAN, vol. 12, p.665.
364e Sabbath, vol. 12, p. 778-782;
364f Sabbath Year, vol. 12, p. 782-3

365 **Archeo-Biblical Egypt.**   Rome 1967, Pontifical Biblical Institute.
180 p.; 3 plans.

365a .. ^RFOHRER G., *Zeitschrift für die alttestamentliche Wissenschaft* 80/1
(Jan.1968) 130.

365b .. ^RCHILDS B., *Journal of Biblical Literature* 87/1 (Mar.1967)
117-118.

Nº 366 **Les fouilles dans la région de Jéricho:** reprints with new charts and plans. Rome 1967, Pontifical Biblical Institute. 156 p.

367 **Color-slide Lectures on Exegesis and Archeology** [= Nº 150 above, with photos improved by Colorvald, Valdagno near Vicenza/Venice], 50 sets of 12 slides each in plastic envelope, with texts and bibliography (revised and reedited → Nº 420). Rome 1967, Pontifical Biblical Institute [abridged tr. by G. TORTA 1989]. Cumulative index volume → 420a. -- First 30 sets 1967:

(1967 Color-slide sets Nº 367): 01 **Via Crucis 1**
: 012 **Via Crucis 2**
: 013 **Jerusalem NE**
: 016 **Temple**
: 017 **Jerusalem W, S**
: 02 **Judah**
: 025 **Samaria**
: 03 **Galilee**
: 035 **Genesareth**
: 04 **OT Excavation**
: 043 **NT Excavation**
: 044 **Qumran Find**
: 045 **Qumran Dig**
: 05 **Petra**
: 055 **Phoenicia**
: 057 **North-Syria**
: 06 **Babylonia**
: 066 **Persia**
: 07 **NT Egypt**
: 072 **Pyramids**
: 073 **Amarna**
: 074 **Luxor**
: 075 **Ramesses**
: 076 **Elephantine**
: 077 **Sinai Route**
: 078 **Sinai**
: 08 **Hittites**
: 09 **Cilicia**
: 093 **Apocalypse**
: 097 **Greece**

368 WINTON THOMAS D., ed., *Archaeology and Old Testament Study* (Oxford 1967): ᴿ*Biblica* 49/1 (Jan.1968) 162-167.

369 God is What we Believe In, *American Ecclesiastical Review* 158/3 (Mar.1966) 160-178.

370 KELLERMANN U., *Nehemia, Quellen, Überlieferung und Geschichte*: BZAW 102; Berlin 1967: ᴿ*Catholic Biblical Quarterly* 30/2 (Apr.1968) 263-266.

371 Secularization of and by the Gospel, *Catholic Commission on Intel-lectual and Social Affairs Meeting*, St.Louis, May 5,1968, p. 13-47.

372 Historiographia exegeseos americanae [R. GRANT]. *Verbum Domini* 46 (1968) 88-98.

373 High Points of Mesopotamian Art, *Orientalia* 37/2 (Apr.1968) 220-231
reviewing:
373a MOORTGAT Anton, *Die Kunst des alten Mesopotamien* (Cologne 1967). &

373b PARROT André, *Mari 3. Temples d'Ishtarat et de Nini-Zaza* (Paris 1967)

373c NISSEN H.-J., *Zur Datierung des Köningsfriedhofs von Ur* (Bonn 1968).

373d NAGEL W., *Die neuassyrischen Reliefstile unter Sanherib und Assurbanaplu* (Berlin 1967).

373e BERAN Thomas, *Die hethitische Glyptik von Boğazköy* (Berlin 1967) – all pp.220-231.

374 The Scotist Cosmic Christ (< N° 336, TEILHARD), in *De Doctrina Ioannis Duns Scoti*, Acta Congressus Oxonii 1966 (Rome 1968) 3, p. 169-217.

Nº 375 SOGGIN J. A., *Das Königtum in Israel* (BZAW 104; Berlin 1967): [R]*Catholic Biblical Quarterly* 30/3 (Jan.1968) 476-478.

375a Tradition in Spirituality, in KESSLER M., ed. TEILHARD symposium *Dimensions of the Future* (Washington 1968, Corpus Books) 22-50 & 191-193.

375b TEILHARD Rocking the Boat of Theology, in symposium *Modern Theological Thinkers,* ed. Thomas E. BIRD (Notre Dame 1968).

376 Do House-Organs or News-Media Best Serve the Christ-Rebel? on Marquette *Tribune* coverage of student-protest riots, May 1968.

376a BAGATTI Bellarmino, *Gli scavi di Nazaret I. dalle origini al secolo XX*: Pubblicazioni dello Studium Biblicum Franciscanum 17 (Jerusalem 1967): [R]*Biblica* 49/2 (Apr.1968) 271-273.

377 MYERS J.M., *The World of the Restoration* (Englewood Cliffs 1968): [R]*Catholic Biblical Quarterly* 30/4 (Oct.1968) 631-632.º

378 BRÄNDLE Max, Did Jesus' Tomb Have to be Empty?, digest (and others anonymously), *Theology Digest* 16/1 (Spring 1968) 18-26, and other issues.

378a Leviticus, in *Encyclopaedia Britannica,* ed BENTON W. (Chicago 1968, University) vol.13, p.1004-1006.

379 Chronicles (-Ezra-Nehemiah); Archeology; (outside Palestine) Geography, in *The Jerome Biblical Commentary*, ed. BROWN R.E., *al.* (Englewood Cliffs 1968, Prentice-Hall), vol.1, p.402-428 = #24,1-14; vol.2, p.653-670 = #74,1-94; p.634-9 = #73.5-31.

379a *Comentario Bíblico "San Jerónimo"* (Madrid 1971-2, Cristiandad) vol. 2, p.173-272; vol.5, p.397-443 & 349-360.

379b *Grande Commentario Biblico* (Brescia 1973, Queriniana), p. 515-583 & 1678-1702 & 1653-1658.

380 Soul-Body Unity and God-Man Unity, *Theological Studies* 30/1 (Mar.1969) 27-60.

381 Recent Christology and Theological Method, *Continuum* 6/1 (Winter 1969) 63-77.

N° 380 + 381 were published as **In Search of the Human Jesus** (Corpus 1969 = N° 408 below, without informing the author).

382 ZIMMERLI W., *Der Mensch und seine Hoffnung im Alten Testament* (Göttingen 1968): [R]*Catholic Biblical Quarterly* 31/1 (Jan.1969) 143-143.

382a Creation, in *Encyclopedia Americana* (1969 ? Not in 1991 edition).

383 BUCCELLATI G., *Cities and Nations of Ancient Syria* (Rome 1967): [R]*Catholic Biblical Quarterly* 31/2 (Apr.1969) 246-247.

383a Angel-Prophet [messenger] or Satan-Prophet [nonconformist] ?, *Zeitschrift für die alttestamentliche Wissenschaft* 91/3 (Jul.1969) 31-87.

384 RODRÍGUEZ MOLERO F., al., *La Sagrada Escritura por profesores de la Compañía de Jesús, II. Conquista de Canaán y monarquía* (Madrid 1968): [R]*Biblica* 50/3 (Jul.1969) 436-438.

385 BRINKMAN J., *A Political History of Post-Kassite Babylonia* (Rome 1968): [R]*Catholic Biblical Quarterly* 31/3 (Jul.1969) 403-404.

386 MANCINI I., *Le scoperte archeologiche sui Giudeo-Cristiani* (Assisi 1968): [R]*Catholic Biblical Quarterly* 31/4 (Oct.1969) 583-584.

387 SELLERS O., *The 1975 Excavation at Beth-Zur*, & KELSO J., *The Excavation of Bethel*: AASOR 38 & 39, 1968: [R]*Biblica* 50/4 (Oct.1969) 554-555.

Nº 388 CHARY T., *Aggée-Malachie* (Paris 1969): [R]*Biblica* 50/4 (Oct.1969) 562–5

389 **Exégèse pratique des petits prophètes postexiliens, bibliographie commentée.** Rome 1969, Biblico, 228 p.

390 **Prophets for the 21st Century.** Rome 1969, Pontifical Gregorian University. 80 p.

390a **Prophetae VT pro exeunte saeculo XX.** Rome 1969, Gregorian. 80 p.

391 **De Jesu Nave; introductio in librum biblicum Yehošua˙ Ben-Nûn.** Rome 1969, Biblico. 64 p.

392 OATES D., *Studies in the Ancient History of Northern Iraq* (London 1968): [R]*Orientalia* 38/4 (Oct.1969) 579-580.

393 JIDEJIAN N., *Byblos through the Ages* (Beirut 1968): [R]*Orientalia* 38/4 (Oct.1969) 584-585.

394 MERRILLEES R., *The Cypriote Bronze Age Pottery Found in Egypt* (Lund 1968): [R]*Orientalia* 38/4 (Oct.1969) 591-593.

395 NAGEL W., *Frühe Plastik aus Sumer und Westmakkan & Berliner Jahrbuch für Vor- und Frühgeschichte* (Berlin 1968): [R]*Orientalia* 38/4 (Oct.1969) 594-595.

396 MICHAŁOWSKI K., ed., *Études et Travaux* (Warsaw 1968): [R]*Orientalia* 38/4 (Oct.1969) 595.

397 VOLLENWEIDER M., *Catalogue raisonné des sceaux cylindres et intailles* (Geneva 1967): [R]*Orientalia* 38/4 (Oct.1969) 595.

398 ÖZGÜÇ Nimet, *Kaniş Kurumu mühürleri* [seals] (Ankara 1968): [R]*Orientalia* 38/4 (Oct.1969) 596.

399 KYRIELEIS M., *Throne und Klinen* (Berlin 1969): [R]*Orientalia* 38/4 (Oct.1969) 597.

400 VANDEN BERGHE L., *Opgravingen i Pusht-i Kuh* (Brussels 1968): [R]*Orientalia* 38/4 (Oct.1969) 597-598.

401 KLEINER G., *Die Ruinen von Milet* (Berlin 1968): [R]*Orientalia* 38/4 (Oct.1969) 598.

402 Biblioj, sed je kia prezo? [l3th century cost of one Bible, £1: = one year's salary], [R]*Biblia Revuo* 5/5 (Nov.1969) 279-296.

403 Saecularismus in revelatione biblica, on FIOLET H., *Vreemde verleiding,* & NIJK A., *Secularisatie* (Rotterdam 1968): *Verbum Domini* 47/4 (Dec.1969) 215-224.

404 The Geographical Setting of Biblical History, p.68-74 = #53-58; Archaeology and the Bible, p.93-104 = #77-84; Measures, Weights, Money and Time, p.105-108 = #86-87; The Critical Study of the Old Testament, p.225-123 = #91-97: in [²] *New Catholic Commentary on Holy Scripture*, ed. FULLER R.: London 1969, Nelson.

405 ALBRIGHT W. F. volume, ed. MALAMAT A., *Eretz Israel Annual* 9 (Jerusalem 1969) :[R]*Journal of Biblical Literature* 88/4 (Dec. 1969) 474-477.

406 HART R., *Unfinished Man and the Imagination* (New York 1968): [R]*The Modern Schoolman* 47 (Jan.1970) 244-248.

407 **History of Biblical Criticism**, volume commissioned for a Corpus Instrumentorum *Catholic Theological Encyclopedia* but never published.

408 **In Search of the Human Jesus** [= N° 380-381 above, without informing the author]. New York 1970, Corpus Papers. 63 p.

409 Zechariah's Seven-Spout Lampstand, *Biblica* 51/2 (Apr.1970) 183-206; 1 plate.

N° 410 GRINTZ Y., *Studies in Early Biblical Ethnology and History* (Tel Aviv 1969): [R]*Biblica* 51/2 (Apr.1970) 277-279; see 52/2 (Apr.1971) 289, "A Rectification" by R. MACKENZIE.

411 Universalismo y segregación postexílica (= N° 343a above), *Semana Biblica Española XXVI 1965* (Madrid 1970) 283-297.

412 BADAWY A., *History of Egyptian Architecture*, 2 vols. to 1085 B.C. Berkeley 1966, 1968): [R]*Orientalia* 39/2 (Apr.1970) 204-205.

413 ALP S., *Zylinder- und Stempelsiegel aus Karahöyük* (Ankara 1968): [R]*Orientalia* 39/2 (Apr.1970) 207.

414 CORBO V., *The House of St. Peter at Capharnaum* (Jerusalem 1969): [R]*Biblica* 51/3 (Jul.1970) 425-426.

415 Centrifugal and Centripetal Tendencies in the Judaic Cradle of Christianity, in A. OTTAVIANI Festschrift *Populus Dei I. Israel* (= *Communio* 10, Rome 1970) 615-651.

N° 416 OTTOSSON M., *Gilead, Tradition and History* (Lund 1969): [R]*Catholic Biblical Quarterly* 32/4 (Oct.1970) 623-5.

417 O'CONNOR D., *Peter in Rome: the Literary, Liturgical and Archaeological Evidence* (New York 1969): [R]*Biblica* 51/4 (Oct.1970) 571-574.

418 SCHILLEBEECKX E., *God the Future of Man*; & *The Eucharist* (New York 1968): [R]*The Modern Schoolman* 47 (Oct.1970) 458-460.

419 Gray's TEILHARD, on D. GRAY, *The One and the Many*: [R]*Continuum* 7/4 (Winter 1970) 631-634.

N° 420 **Rome Biblical Institute Color-Slide Lectures Text & Documentation** [adding **20 sets** to N° 367 (< N° 150) above]
: 01 **Via Crucis** 1971, 12 p.
: 012-**013 Via Crucis 2** 1971, 44 p.
: 015 Northeast Jerusalem 1972, 48 p.
: 016 Jerusalem Temple 1971, 72 p.

N° **420**: 017 Jerusalem west/south 1972, 48 p.
: **019 Israel** 1970, 24 p.
: 02 Judah 1971, 44 p.
: 025 Samaria 1971. 48 p.
: 03 Galilee 1971, 48 p.
: 035 Genesareth 1971, 40 p.
: 04 OT Excavation 1971, 72 p.
: **041 Prehistory** 1974, 72 p.
: 042 + **043** NT Excavation, **Masada**
: 044+045 Qumran, 1971 printed, 32 p.
: **046 Jericho** 1971, 64 p.
: **047 Megiddo** 1973, 55 p.
: **048 Hazor** 1971, 56 p.
: **049 Lachish** 1971, 48 p.
: 05 + **051 Edom**-Petra 1971, 64 p.
[N° 420, color-slides documentation]: **053 Moab** 1972, 80 p.
: **054** + 055 Phoenicia 1974, 84 p.
: **056** + 057 **Damascus**, Syria 1974, 82 p.
: **058 Ugarit** 1973, 72 p.
: **059 Palmyra-Dura** 1974, 56 p.
: 06 Babylonia 1975, 72 p.
: 065 Persia 1975, 40 p.
: 07 NT Egypt 1975, 40 p.
: **071** + 072 **Cairo,** Pyramids 1975, 48 p.
: 073 Amarna, 1971 printed, 12 p.
: 074 + **0741** Luxor, **Thebes** 1975, 48 p.
: **076** Elephantine 1975, 23 p.
: 075 + 077,078,**079** Ramesses, Sinai route, Sinai: **The Exodus** 1971
    printed, 52 p.
: 08 Hittites 1975, 31 p.
: **088 Troy** 1975. 24 p.
: 09 **Paul's** Cilicia 1971, 28 p.
: 093 + **095** The Apocalypse 1971, 56 p.
: **094 Cappadocia** 1975, 24 p.
: 097 Greece 1975, 24 p.
420a **Cumulative Index to all slides, booklets, and sources cited.**
    Rome 1976, 244 p.
420b .. abridged in Italian as **Diapositive bibliche** by G. TORTA
    (seminary,1989).

N° 421 **Stratigraphia geobiblica / Biblical Near East Archeology and Geography** [= N° 50 + 308 + 125 above, updated and with cumulative index]. Rome 1970, Pontifical Biblical Institute. 351 p.

422 **Tubinga neotestamentaria,** excerpta ex historia exegeseos criticae 1. Rome 1971, Biblical Institute. 48 p.

423 **Reges**: Introductiones speciales in V.T. libros, 3 [1 & 2 = N° 343 & 391 above]. Rome 1971, Biblical Institute. 200 p.

N° 424 Phoenicia-Canaan Frontier *L^ebô'* of Hama, *Mélanges de l'Université Saint-Joseph de Beyrouth* 46 (second M. DUNAND issue, 1971) 69-103.

425 New Frames for Near East Archeology, *Orientalia* 40 (1971) 341-354;

bulletin:

425a EDWARDS I., ed., *Cambridge Ancient History*[3] 1/1, 1970: [R]341.

425b MADHLOOM T., *Chronology of Neo-Assyrian Art* (London 1970) 346.

425c MALLOWAN M. & DAVIES L., *Ivories in Assyr-ian Style* (London 1970): [R]347.

425d STROMMENGER E., *Die neuassyrische Rundskulptur* (Berlin 1970): 348.

425e LENZEN H., *XXIV. Bericht Uruk/Warka 1965-6* (Berlin 1968):348

425f BIVAR A., *Catalogue of the Western Asiatic Seals* (British Museum 1969) 348-9.

425g CALMEYER P., *Datierbare Bronzen aus Luristan und Kirmanshah* (Berlin 1969): 349.

425h HINZ W., *Altiranische Funde und Forschungen* (Berlin 1969): 349.

425i ERDMAN K., *Kunst Irans* (Mainz 1969) 349.

425j NAPOLEONE-LEMAIRE J., *L'église à atrium*, <u>Apamée</u> 1/1 (Brussels 1969): 349.

425k BALTY J., *Triclinos & Bilan 1965-8*, <u>Apamée</u> Miscellanea 2 & 6 (Brussels 1968): 360.

425L RIIS P., *Sūkās I* (Copenhagen 1970): 350

425m WOOLLEY C., *Carchemish I-II* (London 1969 = 1914-21):351.

425n JIDEJIAN N., *Tyre through the Ages* (Beirut 1969): 351.

425ö SCHÜLE W., *Meseta-Kulturen* (Berlin 1969): 351.

425p NIEMEYER H., *Toscanos* (Berlin 1969): 352.

425q MOOREY P., *Archaeology, Artefacts and the Bible* (Oxford 1969): 182.

425r NEGBI O., *The Hoards of Goldwork from Tell el-'Ajjûl* (Göteborg 1970):352.

425s KENNA V., *Cretan Talismanic Stone* (Lund 1969): 352.

425t SCHWARTZ J., *Qaṣr-Qarun* (Cairo 1969): 352.

425u LLOYD S., *Beycesultan* (London I 1962, II 1965): 353.

425v ÖZGÜÇ T., *Altıntepe* (Ankara 1966): 353.

425w SCHIRMER W., *Bebauung Büyükkale-Boğazköy* (Berlin 1969):353.

426 BUSINK T., *Der Tempel von Jerusalem I. Salomos* (Leiden 1970): [R]*Biblica* 52/3 (Jul.1971) 446-448.

N° 427 SOGGIN J.A., *Le livre de Josué* (Neuchâtel 1970): [R]*Biblica* 52/3 (Jul. 1971) 448-449.

428 Pannenberg's Historicizing Exegesis, *Heythrop Journal* 12/4 (Oct.1971) 377-400.

428a .. (should have stressed TROELTSCH more): R. RUBANOWICE, *Heythrop Journal* 13/4 (Oct.1972) 436-441.

429 STADELMANN L., *The Hebrew Conception of the World* (Rome 1970): [R]*Catholic Biblical Quarterly* 33/3 (Jul.1971) 464-465.

430 BERNHARDT K., *Die Umwelt des Alten Testaments I*[2] (Berlin 1968): [R]*Biblica* 52/4 (Oct.1971) 581-592.

431 Byblos and Jericho Neolithic Floors, *Fifth Congress of Jewish Studies 1969* (Jerusalem 1972) vol.1, p. 35-49.

432 Prophecy to Apocalyptic via Zechariah: Uppsala OT Congress 1970: *Vetus Testamentum Supplement* 22 (1972) 47-71,

433 [R]BEIJER ., *Pauli värld och verk* (Stockholm 1971): [R]*Credo*, Uppsala 53 (1972) 139.

434 Myth and Reality in Scripture, *The Jesuit* (Wisconsin Spring 1972) 11-17.

435 Civil Authority in Ezra, *Studi in onore di E. VOLTERRA* (Milan 1972), vol,6, p.377-402 (reprinted in N° 577 below, AnB 142, p,107-134.

436 DE MIROSCHEDJI P., *L'Époque pré-urbaine en Palestine* (Paris 1971): [R]*Catholic Biblical Quarterly* 34/2 (Apr.1972) 234-235.

437 CASTELLINO G., ed., *Storia delle religioni*[6] (Torino 1971): [R]*Orientalia* 41/2 (Apr.1972) 303-305.

438   LOMBARDI G., *Tomba di Raḥel* (Jerusalem 1971): [R]*Biblica* 53/3 (Jul.1972) 421-422.

439   GOODCHILD R., *Kyrene and Apollonia* (Zürich 1971}: [R]*Orientalia* 41/3 (Jul.1972) 451.

440   HAINES R., *Excavations in the Plain of Antioch II* (Chicago 1971): [R]*Orientalia* 41/3 (Jul.1972) 451-452.

441   STÈVE M., *L'Acropole de Suse* (Leiden 1971): [R]*Orientalia* 41/3 (Jul.1972) 452.

442   MELLOR E. & LACE O., *The Making & The Understanding of the Old Testament* (Cambridge 1972): [R]*Review for Religious* 31/6 (1972) 1075-6.

443   DE VAUX R., *Histoire ancienne d'Israël I-II* (Paris 1971. 1973): [R]*Theological Studies* 33/4 (Dec.1972) 748-750 & 35/4 (Dec.1974) 734-735.

444   Bibliography of Works in Theology and History, *History and Theory* 12/1 (1973) 55-140.

445   The Hivites [in table of varyingly-ordered pre-Israel occupants of Canaan], *Biblica* 54/1 (Jan.1973) 43-62.

446   SCHALIT A., *König Herodes* (Berlin 1969): [R]*Biblica* 54/1 (Jan.1973) 122f

447   Rozwój archeologiczno-egzegetyczny   25 lat, *Ruch Biblijny i Liturgiczny* 26/2 (1973) 57-67.

448   <u>Ugarit</u> Grid, Strata, and Find-Localizations, *Zeitschrift des Deutschen Palästina-Vereins* 89 (1973) 113-150.

448a .. wrongly situates a whole recent excavation-area now [for the first time] published in J. COURTOIS, Ugarit Grid, Strata, and Find-Localizations: a Reassessment, *ZDPV* 90 (1974) 97-114.

449   FERNÁNDEZ N., *Anotaciones críticas al texto griego del Génesis* (Madrid 1972): [R]*Catholic Biblical Quarterly* 35/2 (Apr. 1973) 236-237.

450   ORLINSKY H., *Understanding the Bible through History and Archaeology* (New York 1962): [R]*Catholic Biblical Quarterly* 35/2 (Apr. 1973) 261-263.

451   YEIVIN S., *The Israelite Conquest of Canaan* (Istanbul 1971) [R]*Biblica* 54/2 (Apr. 1973) 289-291.

452 . GUNNEWEG A., *Geschichte Israels bis Bar Kochba* (Stuttgart 1972): [R]*Biblica* 54/3 (Jul. 1973) 443-444.

453 **Recent Reformulations of the Mystery of Christ** (class-lectures on N° 380 & 381 above). Windsor 1973, University. 16 p.

454   DOTHAN M., *Ashdod II-III - Atiqot* 9-10 (Jerusalem 1971): [R]*Biblica* 54/4 (Oct. 1973) 564-566.

455   WILLI T., *Die Chronik als Auslegung* (FRLANT 106, Göttingen 1972): [R]*Catholic Biblical Quarterly* 35/4 (Oct. 1973 565-566.

456 Fosoj de Jeriho kai ekzegezo de la Biblio, *Biblia Revuo* 9/4 (Oct. 1973) 215-232.

457 **Theology Digest Index volumes 1-20, years 1953-1972.** Saint Louis University 1974, School of Divinity.

458   BOTTERWECK G., *al.* ed., *Theologisches Wörterbuch zum Alten Testament* → 552; tr. 552a..

459 Does Archeology Prove Chronicles Sources?, in MYERS J. Festschrift *A Light unto my Path* (Philadelphia 1974) 375-401.

460 New Light on Ancient Records, *Orientalia* 43/2 (Apr.1974) 237-251; bulletin:

460a POSNER E., *Archives in the Ancient World* (Harvard 1972): [R]p.237.

460b OPPENHEIM A., *al.*, *Glass and Glassmaking in Ancient Mesopotamia* (Corning NY 1970): p. 239.

460c BOESE J., *Altmesopotamische Weihplatten* (ZA Ergnzungsband 6): p. 240.

460d ELLIS R., *Foundation-Deposits in Ancient Meso-potamia* (New Haven 1968): p. 241.

460e AMIET P., *Glyptique ancienne des origines à l'époque des Perses achéménides* (Paris 1972): p.242.

460f MOORTGAT-CORRENS U., *Bildwerke vom Djebelet el Beda* (Berlin 1972): p.243.

460g HELLSTRÖM P., *Sudanese Nubia: Rock Drawings*; MARKS A., *Preceramic Sites*; GARDBERG C., *Late Nubian Sites*; NIELSEN O., *Human Remains* (Stockholm, all 1970): p.244-5.

460h MOSTAFA S., *Moschee des Farağ ibn Barquq in Kairo* (Glückstadt 1972): p. 245.

460i HUARD P., *Problèmes archéologiques entre le Nil et le Sahara* (Cairo 1972): p. 245.

460j YADIN Y., *Hazor*: Schweich Lecture 1970 (London 1972): p. 246.

460k BEN-SHEM I., *Kibbuş `Eber ha-Yarden* (Tel Aviv 1972): p. 247.

460L KISTER M., *al.*, *Israel Oriental Studies I* (Tel Aviv 1971): p. 247.

460m DE MEYER L., *Tell ed-Dēr* (Louvain 1971): p. 248.

460n DUNANT G., *Le sanctuaire de Baalshemin à Palmyre 3. Les inscriptions* (Rome 1971): p.248.

[N° 460, New Light] ö SCHAEFFER-DE CHALON I., ed., *Alasia: XXe campagne de fouilles à Enkomi* (Paris 1971): p. 249.

460p ERGÜLEÇ H., *Corpus of Cypriote Antiquities 4. Istanbul* (Göteborg 1972): p. 250.

460q OVERBECK J., *Two Cypriot Bronze Age Sites at Kafkallia (Dhalli)* (Göteborg 1972): p. 250.

460r SYMEONOGLOU S., *Kadmeia I* (Göteborg 1973)250.

460s JANTZEN U., *Ägyptische und orientalische Bronzen aus dem Heraion von Samos* (Bonn 1972): p.251.

461 Yom Kippur and the Jubilee Year of Reconciliation: St.Louis University 1975 Hillenbrand Lecture: *Theology Digest* (unabridged) 22/4 (Winter 1974) 346-359 [tr. El Yom Kippur, in *Colligite* 21 (León 1975) 382-391].

462 The Holy Year and the Jubilee, *Sidic* 7 (1974) 12-16.

463 SCHÜRER E., [2]VERMES G., *The History of the Jewish People in the Age of Jesus Christ* (Edinburgh 1973): [R]*Biblica* 55/4 (Oct.1974) 569-571.

464 LARSSON G., *The Secret System* [OT chronology] (Leiden 1973): [R]*Theological Studies* 35/4 (Dec.1974) 584-585.

465 MOSIS R., *Untersuchungen zur Theologie des chronistischen Geschichtswerkes* (Freiburg 1973): [R]*Biblical Theology Bulletin* 4/3 (Oct.1974) 332-6.

466 MYERS J. Festschrift, (→ N° 459) *A Light unto my Path* (Philadelphia 1974): [R]*Review for Religious* 34/1 (1975) 167.

467 Problemi cruciali della storia biblica (-archeologica-geographica) & Alcuni esegeti ed archeologi spesso citati & Cartine I-VIII, in MARTINI C. & PACOMIO Ł., ed., *I libri di Dio: introduzione generale alla Sacra Scrittura* (Torino 1975) 337-494 & 619-636 & 671.

468 ALLEN L., *The Greek Chronicles*: VTS 25 & 27 (Leiden 1974): [R]*Catholic Biblical Quarterly* 37/2 (Apr. 1975) 239-240.

469 Jeroboam's Tragic Social-Justice Epic, *Homenaje a Juan* PRADO (Madrid 1975) 191-214.

470 SANDMEL S., *The Enjoyment of Scripture* (London 1972): [R]*Theologische Literaturzeitung* 100/8 (Aug.1975) 587-588.

471 Iran's New Continuing Encyclopedia: on *Commémoration Cyrus I*, ed. DUCHESNE-GUILLEMIN J., Acta Iranica 1-2 (Tehran 1974): [R]*Orientalia* 44/3 (Jul.1975) 444-446.

472 Is Jesus Man Plus God? & Latin American Liberation Theology, anonymous composite abstracts in *Theology Digest* 23/1 (Spring 1975) 59-70 & 23/3 (Autumn 1975) 241-250.

473 Tin, Gift-Mercantilism: Archeological Varia, *Orientalia* 33/4 (Oct. 1975) 489-401:
　　　　　　　　bulletin:
473a MUHLY J., *Copper and Tin .. in the Bronze Age* (New Haven 1973): [R]p.489.

473b ZACCAGNINI C., *Lo scambio dei doni nel Vicino Oriente sec. 15-13* (Rome 1973): p. 490.

473c MARTIN G., *The Royal Tomb at el-`Amarna I. The Objects* (London 1974): p.491.

[N° 473, Tin ...] d CAMINOS R., *The New-Kingdom Temples of Buhen* (London 1974): p.491.

473e GARDE-HANSEN P., *On the Building of the Cheops Pyramid* (Copenhagen 1974): p.492.

473f MANNICHE L., *Ancient Egyptian Musical Instruments* (Munich 1975): p.492.

473g FLAGGE I., *Untersuchungen zur Bedeutung des Greifen* (Sankt Augustin 1975): p.492.

473h BERG W., *Historische Karte des alten Ägypten* (Sankt Augustin 1973): [R]p. 493.

473i SAUNERON S., *Travaux de l'Institut français d'archéologie orientale 1969-1974* (Paris 1974): p.493.

473j ROSEN-AYALON M., *Ville royale de Suse I. La Poterie islamique* (Paris 1974): p.494.

473k TRUMPELMANN L., *Iranische Denkmäler II/A Sar Mašhad* (Berlin 1975): p.494.

473L NYBERG H., Festschrift, *Acta Iranica* 4-5 (Tehran 1975): p.494.

473m KARAGEORGHIS V., *Cypriote Antiquities in San Francisco* (Göteborg 1974): p.495.

473n MASSON E., *Cyprominoica* (Göteborg 1974): p.495.

473ö ROOS P., *Rock-Tombs of Caunus* (Göteborg 1972-4): p.495.

473p HAMMOND P., *The Nabataeans: their History, Culture and Architecture* (Göteborg 1973): p.495.

473q STEWART J., *Tell Ajjul, Middle Bronze* (Göteborg 1974): p. 495.

473r MERRILLEES R., *Trade and Transcendence in the Bronze Age Levant* (Göteborg 1974): p.496.

473s LONG C., *The Ayia Triadha Sarcophagus* (Göteborg 1974): p.496.

473t PLOUG G., *Sukas* II & RIIS P., *Sukas* III (Copenhagen 1973-4): p.496.

473u BLÁZQUEZ J., *Colonizaciones semitas en Andalucía: Tartessos*[2] (Valencia1975, Salamanca 1975): p.496.

473v DEVER W., *Gezer II* (Jerusalem 1974): p.497.

473w OREN E., *The Northern Cemetery of Beth-Shan* (Leiden 1973): [R]p.498.

473x BEN-TOR A., *Two Burial Caves at Azor: First Season Yarmuth* (Jerusalem 1975): p.499.

473y CAUVIN J., *Religions néolithiques de Syrie-Palestine* (Paris 1972): p.499.

473z DUPONT-SOMMER A. Festschrift (Paris 1971): p.500.

473aa DE SANDOLI S., *Corpus inscriptionum Crucesignatorum* (Jerusalem 1974): p.501.

474 HERRMANN S., *History of Israel* (Munich 1973): [R]*Biblical Theology Bulletin* 6/1 (Feb.1976) 110-112.

475 HARRIS H., *The Tübingen School* (Oxford 1975): [R]*Biblica* 57/2 (Apr.1976) 293-295.

476 *Staurós* nell'archeologia e nel Nuovo Testamento, in *Sapienza della Croce oggi*, Congresso Passionisti 1975 (Rome 1976) vol.1, p.466-481.
476a .. also in *Parole di Vita* 21/2 (1976) 33-54 [= 115-134].
476b .. objections of Emmanuele TESTA, Ma Cristo è poi morto in Croce?, I-XII inserted in *La Terra Santa* 52/10 (Oct.1976) after p.352.
476c .. and of Luigi FOSSATI, "Rifiuto quasi unanime degli esegeti" per la Sacra Sindone ?, *Sindon* (Oct.1976) 31-38.

N° 477 YADIN Yigael, *Jerusalem Revealed 1968-1974* (Jerusalem 1975): [R]*Biblica* 57,2 (April 1976) 256-257.

478 KEEL Othmar, *Wirkmächtige Siegeszeichen im AT* (Fribourg 1974): [R]*Biblica* 57,2 (April 1976) 274-275.

479 *Tabula peutingeriana*, ed. Ekkehard WEBER → 499.

480 ODED B., ed., *Studies in the History of the Jewish People and of the Land of Israel* (Haifa 1974): [R]*Catholic Biblical Quarterly* 38,2 (April 1976) 252-253.

481 Akhenaten Secularized? [on C. ALDRED, *Cambridge Ancient History* 2,2: 49-97]: *Biblica* 58,2 (April 1977) 246-258.

482 Discoveries at Capharnaum [on V. CORBO, *al.*, *Cafarnao* (Jerusalem 1975)], *Biblica* 58,3 (July 1977) 424-431.

483 LAPERROUSAZ E.-M., *Qoumran* (Paris 1976): [R]*Biblica* 58,3 (July 1976) 432.

484 PRITCHARD James B., *The Ancient Near East 2. A New Anthology of Texts and Pictures* (Princeton 1975): [R]*Catholic Biblical Quarterly* 39,2 (April 1977) 267-268.

485 MÖLLER C. & SCHMITT G., *Siedlungen Palästinas nach Flavius Josephus* : TAVO B-14 (Wiesbaden 1976): [R]*Biblica* 58,4 (Oct.1977) 569-570.

486 WÜST M., *Untersuchungen zu ... Ostjordanland*: TAVO B-9 (Wiesbaden 1975): [R]*Biblica* 58,4 (Oct. 1977) 570.

487 RHOADS D.M., *Israel in Revolution .. Josephus* (Philadelphia 1976): [R]*Biblica* 58,4 (Oct. 1977) 570-571.

488 PETROZZI M.T., *Il Monte Tabor e dintorni* (Jerusalem 1976): [R]*Biblica* 58,4 (Oct. 1977) 571-572.

489 BECKER J., *Wege der Psalmenexegese* (Stuttgart 1975): [R]*Theologische Literaturzeitung* 102,12 (Dec. 1977) 878-879.

490 From Raamses to Ur: Excavators' Choices: *Orientalia* 47,1 (Jan. 1978) 114-136;.

bulletin:

490a BIETAK Manfred, *Tell el-Dab`a [Qantîr] II* (Vienna 1975):[R]*Orientalia* p.114-5.

490b BADAWI Alexander, *The Tombs of Iteri, Sekhem`ankh-Ptah and Kaemnofert at Giza* (Berkeley 1976): *Or* p.115-6.

490c EDEL Elmar, *Jahresritenreliefs ... Ne-User-Re* (Berlin 1974): *Or* p.116.

490d WEDGE Eleanor P., ed., *Nefertiti Graffiti: Comments* [of children] *on an Exhibition* (Brooklyn 1976): *Or* p.116.

490e MANNICHE Lise, *Musical Instruments from the Tomb of Tut`ankhamūn* (Oxford 1976): *Or* p.116-7.

490f ANDERSON Robert D., *Musical Instruments* (London 1976, British Museum): *Or* p.117.

490g COONEY John D., *Glass* (London 1976, British Museum): *Or* p.117.

490h GRIMM Günter, *Kunst der Ptolemäer- und Römerzeit im Ägyptischen Museum* (Mainz 1975): *Or* p.117.

490i NEGEV Avraham, *The Inscriptions of Wadi Haggag, Sinai*: Qedem 6 (Jerusalem 1977): *Or* p.117-8.

[N° 490, From Raamses ...]· j VERCOUTTER Jean, *Mirgissa 2-3* (Paris 1975-6): *Rorientalia* 47 (1978) p.118.

490 k VILA André, *al.*, *La Prospection archéologique de la vallée du Nil au sud de la cataracte de Dal 1 & 3-6* (Paris 1995-7): [R]*Orientalia* 47 (1978) p.119.

490L HOFMANN Inge, *Wege und Möglichkeiten eines indischen Einflusses auf die meroitische Kultur* (Bonn 1975): *Or* p.120.

490m HINTZE Fritz, Festschrift *Ägypten und Kusch*, ed. Erika ENDESFELDER, *al.* (Berlin 1977): *Or* p. 120.

490n WOOLLEY Leonard † & MALLOWAN Max, *Ur Excavations 7. The Old Babylonian Period*, ed. T.C. MITCHELL (London 1976): *Or* p.120-121.

490o HROUDA B., *al.*, *Isin 1973-4* (Munich 1977): *Or* p.121-2.

490p ELLIS Maria D., *Agriculture and the State in Ancient Mesopotamia* (Philadelphia 1976): *Or* p.122.

490q WÄFLER Marcus, *Nicht-Assyrer neuassyrischer Darstellungen*: AOAT 26 (Kevelaer/Neukirchen 1975): *Or* p. 122-3.

490r COLLON Dominique, *The Seal-Impressions from Tell Atchana / Alalakh*: AOAT 27 (Kevelaer/Neukirchen 1975): *Or* p.123.

490s,t *Acta Iranica* 12 & [W.B. HENNING reprints] 14-15 (Tehran/Liège 1977): *Or* p.123-4.

490u GURNEY O.R., *Some Aspects of Hittite Religion*: Schweich Lectures 1976 (London 1967): *Or* p.124.

490v KÜHNE Hartmut, *Die Keramik vom Tell Chuēra* (Berlin 1976): *Or* 124f.

490w FELLMANN Rudolf & DUNANT Christiane, *Le Sanctuaire de Baal-shamin à Palmyre 6. Kleinfunde* (Rome 1975, Institut Suisse): *Or* p.125.

490x PARROT André, *L'Archéologie*² (Paris 1976):ᴿ*Or* p.125.

490y HANSEN Henny H., *An Ethnographical Collection from the Region of the Alawites* (Copenhagen 1976): *Or* p.125-6.

490za MEYERS Carol L., *The Tabernacle Menorah* (Missoula 1976): *Or* p.126.

490zb FRITSCH Charles T., ed., *Studies in the History of Caesarea Maritima*: BASOR supp. 10 (Missoula 1975): *Or* p.127.

490zc MEYERS Eric M., *al., Ancient Synagogue Excavations at Khirbet Shema*`: AASOR 42 (Durham 1976, Duke/ASOR): *Or* p.127-8.

490zd AVIGAD Nahman, *Bullae and Seals from a Post-Exilic Judean Archive*: Qedem 4 (Jerusalem 1976): *Or* 128 (& 129).

490ze POUILLOUX J. & ROUX G., *al., Salamine de Chypre, fouilles Univ. Lyon, vol. 1-6* (Paris 1969-75): *Or* p. 130-1.

490zf SIMA: 43: NICOLAU Kyriakos, *The Historical Topography of Kition*, 1976. -- 45/2-3: ÅSTRÖM Paul, *al., Cape Kiti & Excavations*, 1975-7. -- 46: PAPADOPOULOS A.J., *Excavations at Aigion 1970*: 1976. -- 47: ADELMAN C.M., *Cypro-Geometric Pottery*, 1976. -- 48: DOUMAS Christos, *Early Bronze Age Burial Habits in the Cyclades*, 1977. -- 49: DICKINSON O., *The Origins of Mycenaean Civilization*, 1977. -- SIMA-Pocket 2: MURRAY Robert L., Jr., *The Protogeometric Style; the First Greek Style*, 1975. -- 4: LAFFINEUR Robert, *Les vases en métal précieux à l'époque mycénienne*, 1977: *Or* p.131-2 (+ 134, SIMA 51: KILMER M.F., *The Shoulder Bust in Sicily*, 1977).

[N° 490, From Raamses ...] zg CLERC Giséla, *al.*, & GUZZO AMADASI Maria Giulia, *al. Fouilles de Kition II.Objets égyptiens / III.Inscriptions phéniciennes* (Nicosia 1976/7):*Or* p.132-4.

490zh WALBERG Gisela, *Kamares, a Study of the Character of Middle Minoan Pottery*: Boreas 8 (Uppsala 1976): [R]*Ori-entalia* 47 (1978) p. 134.

490zj SACCONI Anna, *Corpus delle iscrizioni in Lineare B, II. vascolari; III. Micene*: Incunabula Graeca 57-58 (Rome 1974): *Or* p.134-5.

490zk BLÁZQUEZ José María, *Diccionario de las religiones prerromanas de Hispania* (Madrid 1975), *Or* 136, also on GARCIA Y BELLIDO Festschrift 1976.

491 DE VAUX Roland, *Qumran Grotte 4* (Oxford 1977): [R]*Biblica* 59/3 (July 1978) 418-419.

492 HAYES J. & MILLER J.M., ed., *Israelite and Judaean History* (Philadelphia) :[R]*Biblica* 59,3 (July 1978) 423-7.

493 JAROŠ K., *Sichem* (Fribourg 1976): [R]*Biblica* 59/3 (July 1978) 427.

494 BROWN Raymond E., *The Birth of the Messiah* (Garden City 1977): [R]*Cross Currents* 17/4 Winter (1977-8) 464-467.

495 **A History of Biblical Map-Making**: TAVO (Tübinger Atlas des Vorderen Orients, Beiheft B-32. Wiesbaden 1979, L. Reichert. xi-177 p.; 20 fig.; 4 color pl.

497 CASERTA N., *Gli Esseni* (Naples 1978, ex-504c): [R]*Biblica* 61,1 (1980) 119-20.

498 Adma, in *Grande Dizionario Enciclopedico UTET* (Torino [4]1984) vol. 1, p. 207 verified: also contracted were Acab, Acra, Adama, Barsabas, Betlemme, Cedron, Gerusalemme monumenti, Gihon, Michmash, Mizpa, Ofel, Ramot, Ribla, Sair, Sichem, Silo, Tekoa, Tempio Gerusalemme, Traconitide [but perhaps for part of other articles].

499 WEBER Ekkehard, *Tabula peutingeriana* (Graz 1976): [R]*Orientalia* 46,1 (1977) 155-7.

500 ➜ 524

501 El Yom Kippur y el año jubilar de la reconciliación [< St. Louis Hillenbrand Lecture 1975, in *Theology Digest* 22/4 (1974) 346-359: ➜ N° 461 above], *Colligite* 21/21 (León Jan.1975) 382-391.

502 Qumranica [... *DBS* 31: → 497, CASERTA N.], *Biblica* 61 (1980) 116-120   [+ bulletin]:

502a MAIER Johann, *Die Tempelrolle* (Munich 1978): [R]*Biblica* 61,1 (1980) 116-7.

502b DELCOR Mathias, *Qumran* (Paris 1978): [R]*Biblica* 61,1 (1980) 118-9.

503 PAGELS Elaine, *The Gnostic Gospels* (NY 1979): [R]*Cross Currents* 29,4 (1979-80) 463-7.

504 SOGGIN J. Alberto, *I manoscritti del Mar Morto* (Rome 1978): [R]*Biblica* 61,1 (1980) 120.

505 SETTON K.M., *A History of the Crusades, 2 & 4* (Madison WI [2]1969 & 1977): [R]*Biblica* 61,4 (1980) 590-5.

506 DONNER Herbert & CUPPERS Heinz, *Die Mosaikkarte von Madaba I. Tafelband* (Wiesbaden 1977): [R]*Biblica* 62,1 (1981) 127-9; 2 fig.

507 DAVIES G.I., *The Way of the Wilderness: a Geographical Study of the Wilderness Itineraries in the OT* (Cambridge 1979): [R]*Biblica* 62,2 (1981) 283-4.

508 FINEGAN Jack, *Archaeological History of the Ancient Middle East* (Boulder 1979): [R]*Biblica* 62,2 (1981) 281-2.

N° 509   The Ghassulian Lacuna at Jericho, in A. HADIDI, ed., *Studies in the History and Archaeology of Jordan I* (Amman 1980) 59-66 / Jordan Archeology Conference at Oxford (March 25-30, 1980), *Orientalia* 50,4 (1981) 415-428.

510   A teologia do cronista [→ 281, *JBL* 82/4 (Oct. 1963] in Erhard GER-STENBERGER, ed., *Deus no Antigo Testamento, coletânea* (São Paulo 1981) 347-366.

511   LANGEVIN Paul-Émile, *Bibliographie biblique 1930-75* (Québec 1978, Univ. Laval): [R]*Theologie und Philosophie* 56/4 (1981) 567-8.

512   RINGGREN Helmer, *Die Religionen des Alten Orients* (Göttingen 1979): [R]*Catholic Biblical Quarterly* 43/1 (1981) 112-3.

513   MAEHLER Herwig & STROCKA Michael V., *Das ptolemäische Ägypten* (Berlin 17.-28. Sept. 1976; Mainz 1981): [R]*Orientalia* 52,3 (1981) 440-441.

514   Can Geography Save J from RENDTORFF ?, *Biblica* 63,1 (1982) 47-55.

515   Franciscan Holy Land Archeologists in Rome (Antonianum exposition, April 27-30, 1982), *Biblica* 63/4 (1982) 592-5.

516   Is there a New Testament Archeology?, in the Settimio CIPRIANI Festschrift *Parola e Spirito,* ed. Cesare MARCHESELLI CASALE (Brescia 1982) 2, 689-721.

517   David's Rise: Sacral, Military, or Psychiatric?: *Biblica* 63/4 (1982) 524-544.

518   Social Dynamics from Saul to Jehu, *Biblical Theology Bulletin* 12 (1982) 109-119.

519 MALAMAT Avraham & EPH'AL Israel, *The Age of the Monarchies*: World History of the Jewish People 1/4/1 (Jerusalem 1979): [R]*Biblica* 63/3 (1982) 281-2.

520 THIERING Barbara E., *Redating the Teacher of Righteousness* (Sydney 1979): [R]*Biblica* 63/1 (1982) 117-8.

521 OTTO Eckart, *Jakob in Sichem*: BWANT 110 (Stuttgart 1979): [R]*Biblica* 63/3 (1992) 441-2.

522 THOMPSON Thomas L., *The Settlement of Palestine in the Bronze Age*: TAVO B-34 (Wiesbaden 1979): [R]*Biblica* 63/3 (1992) 442-3.

523 VAN DER LUGT Pieter, *Strofische structuren in de Bijbels-Hebreeuwse poëzie* (Kampen 1980) [R]*Catholic Biblical Quarterly* 44 (1992) 655f

524 Recent Archeology, *Orientalia* 51,1 (1982) 39-48;
                                        bulletin:
524a STEINMEYER-SCHAREIKA Angela, *Das Nilmosaik von Palestrina und eine ptolemäische Expedition nach Äthiopien*: Diss. Klassische Archäologie 10. Bonn 1978, Habelt. 168 p.; 4 pl.; 60 fig.: *Or* p.39-40.

524b SCHNEIDER Hans D.. *Shabtis [Leiden], I. An Introduction to the History of Ancient Egyptian Funerary Statuettes. II. Catalogue. III. Illustrations.* Leiden 1977, Rijksmuseum. xxv-367 p.; v-276 p., pl. 80-138; pl. 1-79, 40 fig. *Or* p. 40-41.

524c VANDIER J., *Manuel d'archéologie égyptienne VI. Bas-reliefs et peintures. Scènes de la vie agricole à l'Ancien et au Moyen Empire.* Paris 1978, Picard. vii-354 p.; 110 fig. *Or* p.41-42.

524d KAPLONY Peter, *Die Rollsiegel des Alten Reichs I. Allgemeiner Teil mit Studien zum Königtum des Alten Reichs*: Monumenta Aegyptiaca 2, Bruxelles 1977, Fond. Reine Élisabeth. xii-380 p. *Or* p.42.

N° 524 (Recent Archeology) e: DOTHAN Trude, *Excavations at the Cemetery of Deir el Balaḥ*: Qedem 10. Jerusalem 1979, Univ. ix-114 p.; 224 fig.: [R]*Orientalia* 51 (1982) p. 42-43.

524f BAR-YOSEF Ofer, al., *Prehistoric Investigations in Gebel Maghara, N. Sinai*: Qedem 7. Jerusalem 1977, Univ. vii-269 p., 113 fig., 19 pl. *Or* p.43.

524g ROSENTHAL Renate, SIVAN Renée, *Ancient Lamps in the Schloessinger Collection*: Qedem 8. Jerusalem 1978, Univ. 179 p.; 697 fig. *Or* p. 43.

524h STERN Ephraim, *Excavations at Tel Mevorakh I. Iron Age--Roman Period*: Qedem 9. Jerusalem 1978, Univ. xiv-105 p.; 31 fig.;46 pl. *Or* 43.

524j ZORI Nehemiah, (Heb.) *The Land of Issachar [... Gilboa]*, *Archaeological Survey*. Jerusalem 1977, Israel Exploration Society. viii-164 p.; 64 fig.; 36 pl. *Or* p.43-44.

524k KENYON Kathleen M., *The Bible and Recent Archaeology*. London 1978, British Museum. 105 p.; 104 fig. *Or* p. 44.

524m BITTEL Kurt, *Beitrag zur Kenntnis hethitischer Bildkunst*: Sitzungsberichte ph/h 1976/4. Heidelberg 1976, Winter. 27 p.; 12 pl. *Or* p.44.

524n THRANE Henrik / ÄLEXANDERSEN Verner, *Sūkās* IV/V. Copenhagen 1978, Munksgaard. *Or* p.44-45.

524p SIMA: 4: ÅSTRÖM Paul, al., *The Cuirass Tomb and Other Finds at Dendra I. The Chamber Tombs*, 1977. -- 20/6: BLIQUEZ Lawrence J., *Cypriote Objects in Washington State*, 1978. -- 45/4: HULT Gunnel, MCCASLIN Dan, *Hala Sultan Tekke*, 1978. -- 53: HIRSCH Ethel S., *Painted Decoration on Floors*, 1977. -- 54: WALDBAUM Jane C., *From Bronze to Iron*, 1978. --- SIMA-Pocket 9: MERRILLEES Robert S., *Introduction to the Bronze Age Archaeology of Cyprus*, 1978. -- 8: HOLMBERG Erik J., *Athens*, 1978. *Orientalia* 51 *(*1982*)* p. 45.

524q GJERSTAD Einar, *Opera minora*, ed. STJERNQUIST Berta, Lund 1977, Gleerup. 8+45+32+43+76 p.; ill. *Or* p. 45-46.

524r HÖLBL Günther, *Zeugnisse ägyptischer Religionsvorstellungen für Ephesus*: ÉPROER 73. Leiden 1978, Brill. xii-94 p.; 16 pl.; 2 plans. *Or* p. 46.

524s JOHANSEN Flemming, *Statues of Gudea Ancient and Modern*: Mesopotamia 6. Copenhagen 1978, Akademisk. 70p.; 121 pl. *Or* 46-47.

524t AL-KHALESI Yasin M., *The Court of the Palms; a Functional Interpretation of the Mari Palace*: Bibliotheca Mesopotamica 8. Malibu 1978, Undena. viii-85 p.; 36 fig.; 6 pl. *Or* p. 47.

524u RITTIG Dessa, *Assyrisch-babylonische Kleinplastik magischer Bedeutung*: Univ. Fachbereich 12, Vorderasien 1. Munich 1977, Uni-Druck. 277 p.; 73 fig.: *Or* p.47-48.

525 BRIEND Jacques & HUMBERT Jean-B., *Tell Keisan*: Orbis Biblicus et Orientalis arch. 1 (Fribourg 1980): [R]*Orientalia* 52,2 (1983) 290-291.

526 (North → 495) *A History of Biblical Map-Making* (TAVO B-32, 1979): [R]*Orientalia* 52/2 (1983) 292-3 (M. OTTOSSON).

527 GÖTTLICHER Arvid, *Materialien für ein Corpus der Schiffsmodelle im Altertum* (Mainz 1978): [R]*Orientalia* 52,2 (1983) 312.

528 DINKLER Erich, *Christus und Asklepios; zur Christustypus der polychromen Platten im Museo Nazionale Romano* (Heidelberg Akad. 1990): [R]*Zeitschrift für Kirchengeschichte* 94 (1993) 119-120.

529 DONNER Herbert, *Pilgerfahrt ins Heilige Land (4.-7. Jh.)* (Stuttgart 1979): [R]*Biblica* 64/1 (1983) 54/1 (1983) 125-6.

N° 530 DE SANDOLI Sabino, *Itinera hierosolymitana crucesignatorum 2*:
SBF 24 (Jerusalem 1980): ^R*Biblica* 54/1 (1983) 126.

531 ZRENNER Claudia, *Die Berichte der europäischen Jerusalempilger
(1476-1524)*: EurHS 1/382 (Frankfurt 1981): ^R*Biblica* 54/1 (1983) 126-7.

532 OTTOSSON Magnus, *Temples and Cult-Places in Palestine*: Boreas 12
(Uppsala 1980): ^R*Biblica* 64/1 (1983) 127-8 [→ *Orientalia* 53 (1984)
129].

533 FINEGAN Jack, *The Archeology of the New Testament World [II.] The
Mediterranean World and the Early Christian Apostles* (Boulder 1981):
^R*Biblica* 64,4 (1983) 571-2.

534 KENYON Kathleen M., ed. HOLLAND Thomas A., *Excavations at Jericho
III* (London 1981): ^R*Biblica* 64,4 (1983) 573-4.

535 Statuary and Surveys, *Orientalia* 53,1 (1984) 125-136;

                                                                Bulletin:
535a SPYCKET Agnès, *La statuaire du Proche-Orient ancien*: HbOr
7/1/2-B (Leiden 1981): *Or* p. 125.

535b LITTAUER M.A. & CROUWEL J.H., *Wheeled Vehicles and Ridden
Animals in the Ancient Near East*: HbOr 7/1/2-B (Leiden 1979): *Or* p.
125-6.

535c TEFNIN Roland, *La statuaire d'Hatshepsut* (Brussels 1919): *Or* p.126.

535d SHINNIE Peter L. & BRADLEY Rebecca J., *The Capital of Kush I. Meroe
Excavations 1965-1972* (Berlin 1980): *Or* p.126-7 [briefly A. VILA,
P.RIIS, P.WAGNER & Palmyra].

535e GENGE Heinz, *Nordsyrisch-südanatolische reliefs* (Copenhagen
1979): *Or* p.128.

535f SERANGELI Flavia, *Insediamento e urbanizzazione nella Palestina del Bronzo Antico* (diss. Rome 1980): *Or* p.128-9 [briefly onLeila BADRE].

535g KEEL Othmar, ed., *Monotheismus im Alten Israel und seiner Umwelt* (Fribourg 1980): *Or* p.130 [others' books on seals, synagogues, Michal, Mishmar, Ebla].

535h WIESSNER Gernot, *Nordmesopotamische Ruinenstätten* [four, all in Turkey] (Göttingen/Wiesbaden 1980): *Or* p.132.

535j BARRELET Marie-Thérèse, ed., *L'archéologie de l'Iraq*: CNRS June 13-15, 1978 (Paris 1980): *Or* p. 132 [133, German of Sylvia MATHESON's Persia guide].

535k SIMA 28, ÅSTRÖM Paul, *Fingerprints* (retrievable from ancient jars, 1980; also SIMA pocket 11); -- 45, ÖBRINK U. & HULT G., 1977-9; -- 52, SIMPSON R., Gazetteer of Aegean 1979; -- 55, PAPADOPOULOS T., *Mycenaean Achaea* 1979; -- 56,58, BETANCOURT P. & KANTA A., Crete 1979,1980; -- 59, JOHNSON Jane, Maroni de Chypre 1980; -- 60, TODD J., *Anatolia Neolithic* 1980; -- 61, MCCASLIN Dan, *Stone Anchors*- - 62: KAPLAN Maureen F., *Origin of Yahudiyya Ware* 1980; -- 63, FISCHER Peter M., *Applications of Technical Devices* (1980); -- SIMA Pocket 10, E. HOLMBERG, *Delphi and Olympia* 1979: *Or* p.134-6.

535m BLÁZQUEZ MARTÍNEZ J.M., *Cástulo III* (Madrid 1981): *Or* p. 136.

535n BETANCOURT Philip P., *The Aeolic Style in Architecture .. Halicarnassus* (Princeton 1977): *Or* p. 136.

536 FITZMYER Joseph A., *To Advance the Gospel* (NY 1981): [R]*Cross Currents* (Spring 1983) 80-82.

537 GALBIATI Enrico R., ALETTI Aldo, *Atlante storico della Bibbia e dell'Antico Oriente* (Milano 1982): [R]*Biblica* 65/4 (1984) 577-8.

N° 538 MEYERS E. & C. & STRANGE J.F., *Excavations at ancient Meiron*: ASOR (Cambridge MA 1981): [R]*Biblica* 65/4 (1984) 579-580.

539 BROWNING Iain, *Jerash and the Decapolis* (London 1982): [R]*Catholic Biblical Quarterly* 46/4 (1984) 744-5.

540 Interpreting the Economy of Salvation; Reconciling Prebiblical, Biblical, and Postbiblical Horizons of Experience, in Francis A. EIGO, ed., *Modern Biblical Scholarship; its Impact on Theology and Proclamation*: Proceedings of Theological Institute N° 16 (Villanova PA 1984) p. 87-123.

541 Violence and the Bible: the GIRARD Connection (CBA presidential address, August 10, 1984), *Catholic Biblical Quarterly* 47/1 (1985) 1-27.

542 COLE Dan P., *Shechem I, the Middle Bronze IIB Pottery*: ASOR (Cambridge MA 1984): [R]*Biblica* 66/3 (1985) 440-441.

543 Quirks of Jordan River Cartography, in A. HADIDI, ed., *Studies in the History and Archaeology of Jordan II* [= 544] (Amman 1983) 213-223; 15 maps.

544 Jordan Paleo-Ecology Congress at Amman [April 4-11, 1983], *Orientalia* 55,3 (1986) 205-235.

545 Ebla Names and Gods at Rome Conference (Università July 15-17, 1985), *Biblica* 67/1 (1986) 137-143.

546 MUSZYŃSKI Henryk & MĘDALA Stanisław, *Archeologia Palestyny w zarysie* (Pelplin 1984): [R]*Catholic Biblical Quarterly* 48/4 (1986) 726s.

547 Symposium on the Mythic in Israel's Origins (Roma Accademia dei Lincei, Feb. 10-11, 1986), *Biblica* 67/3 (1986) 440-448.

548 ... In *International Standard Bible Encyclopedia* (Grand Rapids, Eerdmans):
548a Pergamum, vol.3 (1986) 768-770.
548b Philadelphia, vol. 3 (1986) 830.
548c Sardis, vol. 4 (1988) 336-337.
548d Smyrna, vol. 4 (1988) 555-556.
548e Thyatira, vol. 4 (1988) 846.

549 TUSHINGHAM A.D., [KENYON] *Excavations in Jerusalem 1961-7* (Toronto 1985): [R]*Biblica* 68/3 (1987) 443-5.

550 GIRARD René, *Job, the Victim of his People* (Stanford 1987):[R]*Catholic Biblical Quarterly* 51/3 (1989) 515-7.

551 Yahweh's Asherah, in Joseph A. FITZMYER Festschrift, *To Touch the Text*, ed. Maurya P. HORGAN, Paul J. KOBELSKI (NY 1989, Crossroad) p. 118-137; 4 fig.

552 *d̂rôr & ḥadaš / yôbel / mas & mo'znayim / 'ašer & 'ašan*, in Helmer RINGGREN, *al.*, *Theologisches Wörterbuch zum Alten Testament* (Stuttgart, Kohlhammer) 2 (1977) 283-287 & 759-780 / 3 (1982) 554-560 / 4 (1984) 614-6 &1006-9 / 6 (1989) 423-8 & 438-441.

552a tr. David A. GREEN, *Theological Dictionary of the OT* (Grand Rapids, Eerdmans) *d̂ror* 3 (1978) 265-269 / *ḥadaš* 4 (1980) 225-244 / *yobel* 6 (1990).1-6 / *mo'znayim & mas* 8 (1997) 41-44 & 427-430./..

553 **Elenchus [bibliographicus biblicus] of Biblica**. Rome 1979-99, Pontifical Biblical Institute. Vol. 60 for 1979, with Peter NOBER (†1980): 1982, 1083 p. -- 61 for 1990 (1983) 1295 p. -- 62 for 1981 (1984) 784 p. -- 63 for 1982 (1985) 842 p. -64 for 1983 (1986) 874 p. -- 65 for 1984 (1987) 872p. [The title of Nober's volume 59 was *Elenchus Bibliographicus Biblicus*, as it had been both in volumes 1-58 while it was published as part of the four annual issues of *Biblica*, and after it began with volume 49 for 1968 to be published and sold separately. The addition "of Biblica" was made as a historical

description, not intended as a change of title. The words "bibliographicus biblicus" were at first retained, but gradually omitted as not only superfluous but also confusingly similar to the *Elenchus Bibliographicus* (with large biblical section) of the *Ephemerides Theologicae Lovanienses*.. These steps were contested as a change of title by the Rome Tribunal in 1988, but tolerated on condition of being henceforth published not as an annual but as a "Series" entitled *Elenchus of Biblical Bibliography*. See further J.TRINQUET, Revues bibliques in *Dictionnaire de la Bible Supplement.* 10 (1985) 618-644; col.626, íV. Bibliographies]

553a **Elenchus of Biblica** [now no longer "annual" but "series": Elenchus of Biblical Bibliography 1] for 1985 (1988) 1045 p. -- 2 for 1986 (1989) 869 p. -- 3 for 1987 (1990) 1102 p. -- 4 for 1988 (1991) 1066 p. -- 5 for 1989 (1992) 1092 p. -- 6 for 1990 (1993) 1170 p. -- 7 for 1991 (1994) l062 p.-- 8 for 1992 (1995) 1262 p. -- 9 for 1993 (1995; index camera-ready) 1210 p. -- 10 for 1994 (1997; index camera-ready) 1101 p. – 11 part 2 "Archaeologica-Linguistica-Theologica" for 1995 (1999; entire camera-ready) 954 p. [part 1 "Exegetica" and entire vol. 12 for 1996 (2000) and subsequently by Robert ALTHANN].

554 The Chronicler: 1-2 Chronicles, Ezra, Nehemiah / Biblical Geography 5-36; surrounding countries / Biblical Archaeology (with Philip J. KING), in *New Jerome Biblical Commentary*, ed. Raymond E. BROWN, al. (Englewood Cliffs NJ 1990) 362-398 / 1177-1181 / 1195-1218.

555 Psalm 8 as a miniature of Psalm 104, in Joseph I. HUNT Festschrift, *The Psalms*, ed. J.C. KNIGHT, L.A. SINCLAIR (Nashota WI 1990) 2-10.

556 MAZAR Amihai, *Archeology of the Land of the Bible*: Anchor Bible Reference Library (NY 1990,Doubleday): [R]*Biblica* 72/1 (1991) 137-9.

557 Ezra / Nehemiah / Postexilic Judean Officials [etc.], in *Anchor Bible Dictionary*, ed. David N. FREEDMAN (NY 1992 ➜ 565) 2,726-8 / 4,1058-71 / 5,86-90.

558 KASWALDER Pietro A., *La disputa diplomatica di Iefte*: SBF Analecta 29 (Jerusalem 1990): [R]*Catholic Biblical Quarterly* 54/2 (1992) 325-6.

559 Archeologia e sociologia nella ricerca biblica di fronte al 2000 [conferenza per la fine dell' attività accademica del North 17.XII.1992] in *Acta Pontificii Instituti Biblici* 9/8 (1991s) 735-747 [645-7 presentazione del Rettore K. STOCK].

560 DEMERSON G. & G., *al.*, ed., *Les Jésuites parmi les hommes aux XVI*ᵉ *et XVII*ᵉ *siècles*: Actes du colloque de Clermont-Ferrand, avril 1985: Univ. II,fac. Lettres, NS 25 (1987): [R]*Zeitschrift für Kirchengeschichte* 103 (1992) 268-9

561 Brain and Nerve in the Biblical Outlook, *Biblica* 74,4 (1993) 577-587.

562 CANFORA Luciano, *al.*, ed., *I trattati nel mondo antico; forma, ideologia, funzione*: Saggi storia antica (Roma 1980, Bretschneider): [R]*Catholic Biblical Quarterly* 55/1 (1993) 192-3.

563 Medical Discoveries of Biblical Times, in Philip J. KING Festschrift, *Scripture and Other Artifacts*, ed. M. COOGAN, *al.* (Louisville 1994, Westminster-Knox), p. 311-332; 6 fig.

564 TAPPY Ron E., *The Archaeology of Israelite Samaria I. Early Iron Age through the Ninth Century BCE*: Harvard Semitic Studies 44 (Atlanta 1992, Scholars): [R]*Catholic Biblical Quarterly* 56/2 (1994) 345-6.

565 FREEDMAN David N., *al.*, ed., *Anchor Bible Dictionary*. 6 vols. (NY 1992. Doubleday): [R]*Biblica* 75/2 (1994) 291-5.

566 USSISHKIN D., *Village of Silwan* (Jerusalem 1993): [R]*Biblica* 75/4 (1994) 582-3.

567 State of the Published Proof that Qantîr is Raamses, in Basil HEN-NESSY Festschrift, *Trade, Contact, and the Movement of Peoples in the Eastern Mediterranean*, ed. S. BOURKE, J.P. DESCŒUDRES: Mediterranean Archaeology supp.1 (Sydney 1995) 108-237; map.

N° 568   OSIEK Carolyn, interview (with North) June 17,1995 taped for Catholic Biblical Association, History of Biblical Scholarship Project [p.518-529 in bound Varia 1975-96].

569 Did Ancient Israelites have a Heart ?, *Bible Review* 11/3 (June 1995) p.33; phot.

570 PICCIRILLO Michele, ALLIATA Eugenio, *Umm al-Rasas Mayfa`ah I. Gli scavi del complesso di Santo Stefano*: SBF Collectio Maior 228. Jerusalem 1994, Studium Biblicum Franciscanum. 376 p., xxv plates, 3 plans: [R]*Biblica* 77/2 (1996) 294.

571 FOERSTER Gideon, *Art & Architecture: Masada Final Reports 5* (Jerusalem 1995): [R]*Biblica* 77/4 (1996) 582-4.

572 VAN ECK Gerrit, *Mens en maatschappij tussen chaos en kosmos. Een onderzoek naar fundamenten voor sociale kritiek in de wijs- heidsliteratur in het oude Nabije Oosten en met name in oud Israel* (Meppel 1997, Krips; ix-251 p.) [R]*Catholic Biblical Quarterly* 61/2 (1999) 350-2.

573 BLACKHAM Mark, Tulaylat Ghassul: an Appraisal of Robert North's Excavations (1959-60), *Levant* 31 (1999) 19-64 [North's bound Varia p.19 here adds his letter 31.XII.1999 and diagram dating Ghassul 5500-3800; and after his p.64 GARFINKEL Yosef, "Ghassulian Chalcolithic Presence at Jericho", p.65-69].

574 Maps of the Biblical World, in HAYES John H., ed., *Dictionary of Biblical Interpretation* (Nashville 1999, Abingdon) 2,118-123.

575 BERNETT Monika, KEEL Othmar, *Mond, Stier und Kult am Stadttor: die Stele von Betsaida (et-Tell)*: OBO 161 (Fribourg/Göttingen 1998, Univ./Vandenhoeck & Ruprecht. 175 p.; 121 fig,): [R]*Biblica* 80/3 (1999) 442-3.

576   Could Hebrew have been a Cultic Esperanto?,   *Zeitschrift für Althebraistik* 12/2 (1999) 202-217 [reprinted in N° 577].

577   **Medicine in the Biblical Background, and Other Essays on the Origins of Hebrew**: Analecta Biblica 142.   Rome 2000, Biblical Institute.   192 p.; 2 fig.

578   How Loud was Jesus' Voice ?, *Expository Times* 101,5 (Jan. 2001) 117-120 [reprinted in N° 577].

579   GIBSON E. Leigh, *The Jewish Manumission Inscriptions of the Bosporus Kingdom*: TSAJ 75   (Tübingen 1999, Mohr-Siebeck): R*Catholic Biblical Quarterly* 62/3   (2000) 519-520.

580   **The Biblical Jubilee ... *after fifty years***: Analecta Biblica 145. Rome 2000, Biblical Institute.   167 p.

581   Perspective of the Exodus Author(s), *Zeitschrift für die Alttestamentliche Wissenschaft* (2002) ..

Curriculum Vitae (biographical data)

Robert North, S.J., licentiate in philosophy and theology and M.A. in classics at St. Louis University (N° 2 & 7 above), got his doctorate (N° 72) at the Pontifical Biblical Institute in Rome 1946-51 (with competition-grant of Catholic Biblical Association) and remained there as professor of archeology 1951-94 (emeritus & bibliographer to 2000).

His archeological formation was supplemented by field-work under Kathleen KENYON at Jericho 1952-3, Maurice DUNAND at Byblos 1953, Kurt BITTEL at Boğazköy 1955, and Heinrich LENZEN at Uruk 1956. Then in 1959-60 he directed the continuance of Alexis MALLON's excavation at Teleilat Ghassul (N° 249; also 219, 230, 236, 237, 260, and 523 above).

Besides mid-east archeology and geography he taught at Rome also Arabic and modern Hebrew and Old Testament exegesis. After his *Guide to Biblical Iran* (N° 149), he specialized chiefly in the Persian-influenced postexilic books (N° 379 & 554; also 289, 343, 389, 556).

From 1952 to 1976 he organized annually one or two (sometimes three) study-tours of biblical and archeological sites in Israel/Jordan and the whole Middle East, pioneering in this service at Sinai and in St. Paul's Turkey. Though an indifferent cameraman, at the urging of the participants he began making available color-focusing of the biblical sites, which the tours compelled him to visit repeatedly and in varying conditions of light and accessibility (N° 150 & 420).

From 1956 to 1959 he was director of the branch-house of the Rome Pontifical Biblical Institute in Jerusalem, and his classes there were able to specialize in the Dead Sea Scrolls. The students' examination consisted in reading directly from the ancient texts, at that time available on display in the Hebrew University museum.

From 1960 to 1964 on leave from Rome he spent alternate semesters at Marquette University (associate professor of theology 1963-4) and St. Louis University Divinity School in St. Marys, Kansas.

He was invited to contribute to the *Anchor Bible Dictionary*, *Encyclopaedia Britannica*, *New Catholic Encyclopedia*, *Lexikon für Theologie und Kirche* second edition, *Theologisches Wörterbuch zum Altes Testament*, and *Enciclopedia Biblica* Garriga..

Member of the Catholic Biblical Association and its president in 1984 (N° 541; vice-president in 1969 and 1983) and of the Society of Biblical Literature (executive council 1963-6), he also belonged actively while his duties permitted to: American Schools of Oriental Research, Israel Exploration Society, British Society for Old Testament Study; and less actively to the American Institute of Archaeology, American Oriental Society, National Geographic Society, Catholic Theological Society, and Society of Catholic College Teachers of Sacred Doctrine.

He was guest lecturer at Creighton University, Omaha, 1946; University of Sydney and Canisius College, 1963; University of Melbourne and Catholic Seminary. Melbourne, 1963; Chinese Theologate in Baguio, Philippines, 1963; Seattle University, 1964; Kwang-Ju Seminary, Korea, 1965; Barcelona Theologate, San Cugat, 1964; University of Michigan in Ann Arbor and Windsor University in 1973-4; Gonzaga University, Spokane, 1974; and Sogang University, Seoul, Korea, 1978.

Though assigned again to Seoul for 1980-1 in his province catalogue, with the death of the distinguished thirty-years editor of the *Elenchus Bibliographicus Biblicus*, Peter NOBER, S.J. in 1980, he was asked to continue editing it "provisionally" -- until 2000 (N° 553 & 553a), when he left Rome and the *Elenchus* was taken over by Robert ALTHANN, S.J.

Personal and Family Data

Robert Grady North was born in Iowa City, Iowa, on March 25, 1916. His mother was Veva (for Genevieve) Grady, daughter of two immigrants from Neenah, Ireland. His father, Grenville Paul North, who was a law student there, became a Catholic; he belonged to the tenth generation of a John North of Framingham CT, who arrived there in the 1600s according to his published genealogy.

After "G.P." served in the U.S. Navy in France in World War I, he located the family briefly in Cherokee IA, his birthplace. They moved in 1920 to Omaha NE, where G.P.North headed various successive law firms, and was democratic nominee for U.S. Congress in 1924 († 1957). Two other sons, Grenville jr. (Hicksville NY) and John Edward (later his father's and then others' law partner in Omaha) were born in 1920 and 1925, and were U.S. pilots in World War II; and two daughters, Veva Ann in 1921 (m. Al Elston) and Patricia 1924 (m. Ronald Peterson) both of whom located in Seattle.

Robert North was educated by the Sisters of Mercy in St. Margaret Mary school grades 2-3, by the Sinsinawa Dominican Sisters at St. Cecilia's Cathedral grades 5-8, and by the Jesuits at Creighton Prep 1927-31. He became a Jesuit of the Missouri Province on August 8, 1931, in the novitiate at Florissant; philosophate St.Louis 1936-9; theologate St. Marys Kansas 1941-5; tertianship Cleveland 1945-6.

He taught Greek and Latin at Marquette University High School in Milwaukee 1939-41. Ordained a priest by Bishop Paul Schulte at St.Marys KA on June 21, 1944, he became a member of the Wisconsin Jesuit Province when in 1955 it was divided from Missouri while he was in Rome. Upon terminating his service in Rome in the year 2000 he was assigned to the Milwaukee retirement home for Jesuits in St. Camillus at Wauwatosa.

Mention in minor *Who's Who*s

Relevant data were requested for the following specialized or regional reference works, among others: not verified that they were in all cases actually printed (or sent).

Biblical Archaeology Review volume of archeologists and exegetes. -- *Who's Who in Religion* & *Who's Who in the Midwest* (Marquis: Chicago 60611, 200 E. Ohio St.). -- *American Catholic Who's Who* (Romig:

General Index

Books, AUTHORS, Titles, subjects, Greek/Hebrew *terms,*
others' Books[R], *Periodicals,* antiquity Sites

Scripture Citations in Titles

Genesis

-: 78k 145 296 449 Gn-
Dt: 284 ÷Pentateuch
Gn-Ruth: 85
1-3: 282 283
1,27: 265
2,7: 282 283 333 336
337a,b

Exodus

-: 97 136 150SN 318
581 Ex-Dt -: 78i
15: 312
21,10: 116

Leviticus

-: 34 91 264 301
LevNumDt 96

Numbers

-: 287

Deuteronomy

-: 78i 96 284

Joshua

-: 95 115 125 391 427
451
2,1: 267
3,1: 367
15,9-10: 137

Judges

11,12-28: 558

1 Samuel

-: 117

1 Kings

-: 423 1-2Kgs 341

Chronicles

-: 281 281a 289 334
342 343 358 459 465
468 554 2Chr 455

Ezra

-: 317 334 353 358 435
554 577 &Neh 377

Nehemiah

-: 317 334 353 358 554

Maccabees

1 Mcb -: 206
2 (-4) Mcb -: 206

Psalms

-: 19 191 192 271 489
8: 555
104: 555

Proverbs-Sirach

-: 286

Isaiah

-: 248 357

Jeremiah

-: 231

Habakkuk

-: 78j 105

Haggai

-: 388

Zechariah

-: 532
4,2: 409

Malachi

-: 248 388

Matthew

-: 259

Mark

4,1: 578

Luke

-: 259

Revelation

-: 309
2,13: 16

Periodicals Cited in Bibliography

Finito di stampare
nel mese di giugno 2001

presso la tipografia
"Giovanni Olivieri" di E. Montefoschi
00187 Roma - Via dell'Archetto, 10,11,12